The Hidden WEIGHT Of Ordinary DAYS

The Hidden WEIGHT Of Ordinary DAYS

You'll Find Strength Where You
Were Shattered

Annam M. Gordon

LYNX
PUBLISHERS

© 2025 by Annam M Gordon

ISBN (eBook): 978-1-968012-15-1

ISBN (softcover): 978-1-968012-16-8

ISBN (hardcover): 978-1-968012-17-5

Library Of Congress Catalog Number: 2025916883

Published in the United States of America by Lynx Publishers.

Dedication

To my loved ones, both here and in heaven, your love and loyalty are my armor. To the ones behind the scenes whose support never needed a spotlight and whose faithfulness never demanded to be seen, your presence hits louder than any words. Last but not least, to all who wish to see me on the ground, you should have aimed better. I may stumble sometimes, but I don't fall that easily.

Truth in Plain Language

Not everyone gets a shot at higher education. It's not about intelligence. Some people just never had the chance.
Poverty. Trauma. A system that fails them more often than it helps.

I don't write for self-appointed critics sitting comfortably on the outside. I'm not here to impress anyone who expects poetry in every line, quoting Shakespeare or dissecting metaphors before they take something seriously. But if they do read my work and find something worth their time, I'm truly honored.

I write for people who wake up already in a fight, carrying too much, surviving more than anyone ever should. Shut down.
Scared. Pushed aside. I know what that feels like. So do they.

These are real stories, real struggles. Including mine. In a voice they recognize as their own, which goes straight to the heart and doesn't pretend to be more than it is. A voice that says, "You're not invisible." And, hopefully, when they read my words, it reminds them they matter.

Those are my people, who I'm standing up for. No sugarcoating or fancy edits, just the truth about their life. They trusted me enough to put their feelings into words, to be their voice. I don't take that lightly. So I won't switch up or shrink down to make some other people comfortable. Not now. Not ever.

P.S.

And for the hypocrites, the ones pointing fingers from glass houses: Before you judge, take a long look at the life you're living in the shadows. Check the mess behind your own closed doors. Clean your house before casting judgment on anyone else's. Especially when you don't know the whole story.

Love,
Annam

A Note From My Heart to Yours

Dear You,

If you're holding this book, chances are something inside you has cracked. Or maybe it was broken a long time ago, and you've only just found the courage to look at the pieces.

This book was written in the dark. Not the kind you fix with a light switch, but the kind that settles in your chest and makes you tired of pretending. The words came while I was drowning. I needed something to hold on to; otherwise, I didn't know how to keep breathing.

These words came from deep wounds. Mine and those of strangers, friends, and beautiful souls I've met along the way. From stories we lived and once hid, never thinking anyone would ever see them.

This book isn't just my journey. It is ours.

Even our experiences are different, the ache beneath them often feels the same. The longing to be seen, understood, and finally breathe without fear. I know that ache well. I carried it for too long.
And though that chapter is closed, pain doesn't go away just when we make it through. It wants to be seen.

So I let it speak.

P.S.

There is always a tiny hope. I know you may not believe that right now. That's okay. I didn't either, not at first. But even in your silence or your lowest, someone sees you. Whether you feel it yet or not, there is something sacred in you.

This book isn't a straight path from pain to healing. It is messy. It loops. It slips back. Some days you rise. Some days you don't. That's part of it. Every crack opens a little more and slowly, you begin to come home to yourself.

You are living proof that survival is an art.
And you, my dear,
You are a masterpiece in progress.

Thank you for still being here, breathing with me.

With all my heart,
With you always,
Annam

The Story Behind the Words
From Scars to Sentences

You Called It Weakness. I Made It Power.

I've always loved to write since my childhood. For me, writing isn't just something I do; it's life itself.

Years ago, I had a so-called "friend." We eventually went our separate ways over personal differences.

Back when I was just starting to find my voice as a writer, I showed her some of my early pieces. My beginner "cricks and cracks," as I called them. I admit, they were fragile and messy, grammatically super incorrect. (Still not perfect, but the grammar check app became my best friend.)

Yet, instead of support, she gave me scorn. I still remember her laugh and her words: "Your writing is cheap, cheesy, and depressing. Only miserable, depressed people like you would enjoy them."

It cut me deeply. Especially since at that time, I truly was broken, emotionally, mentally, in every way. But even with the wound her words left in me, I didn't stop. I couldn't. Writing wasn't just something I did; it was how I survived. It was the only way I knew how to breathe. And in time, I proved myself right.

I never imagined that my words would carry enough strength to help heal not just myself, but so many of you. I never could have dreamed that my pain, once poured onto the page, would be something others would hold onto for comfort, as if my words were theirs too. And I certainly could not have fathomed that there would be so many of you seeing yourselves, your lives, in my words and finding solace in what once nearly broke me, realizing you're not alone. I hear you.

And yet, somehow, in some strange, paradoxical way, my brokenness gave me more than I ever asked for. It gave me purpose.
It gave me you.

P.S.

Along the way, some people fail to understand, never did, probably never will, so for them, here is the harsh reality: the depressed, the miserable, they're the ones with a soul truly tested. Dragged through hell, so dark it breaks most people. But they don't turn bitter. They just hold the damage, walk with the wreckage. They've stared into a black hole of suffering so raw it burns through your bones. And still, they don't dump that pain on anyone else.

So let's drop the delusion: depression isn't some rich person's problem or a luxury sickness. It doesn't care about your money, your status, or your lies. When it hits, it shatters everyone. No mercy. No exceptions.

With love, as always,
Annam

The Hurt That Stays

When someone breaks your soul, it is a kind of silence. A wound that doesn't bleed, but stings every time you try to feel something good. But when he breaks your body, too, it becomes something else. He doesn't just hurt you. He changes the way you live inside yourself.

Your body stops feeling like home. Movements that used to be natural tense up. You walk carefully. Sit carefully. Sleep like danger is still in the room and braces for things that aren't happening anymore, it doesn't know the difference between memory and threat.

And you don't see the outing or how to get out. It's like waking up in a maze with no exit, just tight corners and panic. You try to scream, but your voice feels far away. You keep showing up in the world, but it's like being half underwater. Everything muffled and heavy.

You hide your bruises. Pull your sleeves down. Learn how to sit so people won't ask questions. Smile with a split lip. Say you were tired and bumped into the furniture. You tell the same makeup story so many times, by the end its starts to sound true. Cause the real story's too much to say out loud.

Then shame moves in. Slow. Steady. It tells you maybe it wasn't that bad. Maybe you made it worse, and no one would believe you anyway. After a while, it settles in. You stop fighting it. You learn how to hold it without letting it show.

People notice. They ask what made you pull back, why you stay on edge, why you flinch when someone gets too close. You want to explain. Say the truth that your body sees danger everywhere now, that you're buried somewhere deep inside. But nothing comes out. The words stay stuck.

And the worst part is, after a while, you stop looking for a way back. You start to wonder if there ever was one. Maybe this hollow, hurting version of you is all that's left, and it's all there's ever going to be.

The Cost of Staying, the Risk of Leaving

Sometimes, it's not that you don't want to leave.

It's that you can't.
Not right now.
Not yet.

And when people say, "Why don't you just go?" they don't see what "just going" actually means. They don't see the zero dollars in your bank account or the landlord who won't rent to a single mom with no job and two kids clinging to her legs, one baby in her arm.

They miss the fact that the car is in his name, that your phone, your insurance, your entire life is tied to him. They have no idea what it feels like to be this trapped.

They won't hear the kids crying when he slams the door or sit in the silence afterwards when everyone in the house holds their breath. They won't understand that leaving doesn't always mean freedom. Sometimes it means more danger, not less. Restraining orders don't stop fists.

Shelters are full. Courts are slow.

And you're left holding a bag of diapers and a bag of fear, standing in the unknown, wondering where you can go and who you can trust.

You tell yourself you'll wait. One more paycheck. One more month. When they're older. When it's safe.

You bargain with the part of you that still hopes something will change. You make plans in your head while pretending everything is fine. You hide bruises behind excuses, behind long sleeves, behind the words, "It's okay, he's just stressed."

But it's not okay. You know that. Every day you stay chips away at you. At who you used to be. At who you want your children to become. But you're surviving, and that is not nothing. You are protecting them in the only way you know how right now. And when you think about leaving, truly leaving, you are so scared of what he might do. You know how fast a door can turn into a trap. You know how quickly goodbye can become a bruise.

So you wait. Not as you've given up, but making it through is its own kind of strength. And one day, when you are ready, when it is safe, you will leave and no one has the right to judge you for that.

It's not a weakness of yours. It's strategy, survival and in a weird way it's love, twisted up with fear and the weight of a thousand impossible choices.

You Running on Empty Inside

Have you ever wondered why you wake up feeling so tired, even after a full night's sleep? It's not always your body that's worn out. Sometimes your body gets the rest it needs, but your soul doesn't. It carries a weight no amount of sleep can lift. A heaviness that sinks in deep and strikes without warning.

You go to bed early, hoping to feel better by morning, but when your eyes open, it's still there. That ache. That emptiness. That inexplicable fatigue.

Maybe you're missing someone. And deep down, no matter how much you pretend or try to convince the people around you that you don't want them anymore, you do. You're still holding on, care. And you know, no matter what you do, no matter who you're with, you can never feel whole without them.

So you drag yourself through the day, thinking maybe tomorrow will be easier. Thinking maybe a little more rest will help. But the truth is, it's not about sleep. It's about everything you've been holding in, pushing down, pretending it doesn't hurt.

And that kind of tired that no pillow, no nap, no early night can fix.

Love Meets Nonsense
A Recipe for Confusion

When your heart overflows with genuine love, it tends to baffle those whose pockets are stuffed with nonsense. It's like bringing a bouquet to a battle of who can grow the biggest ego. While you're offering roses, they're tossing rotten tomatoes. Love is a language spoken in kindness and truth, but some folks only know the dialect of confusion and pretense.

You see, when you radiate warmth and compassion, it's like trying to shine a flashlight in a cave full of shadows. They don't know where to look, and sometimes, they just want to hide in the dark. It's not that love is complicated; it's that nonsense isn't built for clarity. It's like trying to tune a guitar with rubber strings.

So, if you're handing out empathy and receiving puzzled stares, just remember: you're the chef serving a five-star meal while they're stuck microwaving leftovers. Stay generous with your love; let it be the punchline to their confused jokes. In the end, while they're busy juggling baloney, you're savoring the real deal.

Healing Hurts Too

How do you begin to heal when all the wounds inside you still murmurs their name every time the world grows still, when the stillness isn't peace but a haunting that slips in through the cracks of your strongest hours?

It isn't really the silence that keeps you awake at night. It's the way they echo through everything: the places you once wandered together, the way their laughter still lives in the corners of your mind and all the words you never had the chance or the courage to say.

People say healing just needs time. Like the hours know how to mend what broke. But the days don't bring peace. They loop around and drag pieces of the past with them, sharp ones that still know their name. You don't even have to look for them they show up pulling at places you thought had gone numb.

You try to move forward, to live. But everywhere you go, you stumble into the remains of what was, and instead of comfort, those memories feel like carefully disguised traps, waiting to remind you that the ache hasn't left. It has only gotten better at hiding.

You smile in front of others. You laugh at the right moments. You carry yourself like someone who has let go, but the truth is, that smile never quite reaches your chest. The place where the ache still breathes, where their name still drifts like a ghost that refuses to be exorcised.

You tell yourself you want to forget, that you're done hoping, done wondering if they ever think about you, but even on your strongest days, some small, stubborn part of you still wishes they would pause just once and feel a flicker of what you still carry: the ache, the beauty, the realness of what you once shared.

So, again. How do you heal, really, when every part of what broke you still feels like theirs, still echoes what they did, still holds out for them to make it right?

You don't heal the way people say you will. For you it feels messy and slow and most days, it doesn't even feel like healing.

So, you just keep waking up with it still there till one day, it hurts different.

Not gone or fixed but not running the whole show anymore. And maybe that's as close as it gets for now.

The Truth You Carry

You finally came to peace, not from being understood by others but from no longer letting their twisted version of you define who you are.

They can spin stories however they want, rewrite the past to shut up guilt, convince others of a version, twist you into whatever makes them feel right about what they did. That's their choice and their burden to carry.
Let them paint you in whatever shade helps them sleep at night.

Nobody can erase the grace you showed.
You offered respect when it was never returned, even when they disrespected you publicly.

You were strong enough to choose integrity over retaliation and stayed grounded when striking back would have been easier.
No distortion. No noise. No crowd of supporters or silent haters can alter the truth you carry.

That truth is yours. Solid. Clear. Untouchable.
It lives outside their reach. Doesn't need to be seen to be true.

When Family Becomes the Enemy

There's no pain like the one that comes when family turns into strangers. Not just strangers, but enemies. People who once held your hand now point fingers. The ones who used to protect you are the ones pushing you away.

It's a unique kind of heartbreak, one that doesn't bleed on the outside but eats you alive on the inside.

You grow up believing family means forever, that no matter what, you'll have a place where you're safe, where you're loved unconditionally. But sometimes, the people who are supposed to love you the most are the ones who hurt you the deepest.

It starts small: silent treatments, backhanded comments, moments when you realize their love depends on who they want you to be, not who you are. And then it grows.

Into betrayal. Into resentment. Into something so unfamiliar, you no longer recognize the faces at the table.

You try to hold on. You try to fix it. You tell yourself it's just a phase, that it will go back to how it used to be. But sometimes it doesn't. Sometimes the people you'd do anything for would rather watch you break than bend for you even once.

And that's when you understand: blood doesn't equal loyalty. Family isn't just DNA. It's love, respect, and showing up when it matters. When those things disappear, you have to protect your peace, even if it means walking away from the people who gave you your name.

It hurts. God, it hurts. But healing begins where pretending ends. And the bravest thing you can do is let go of what's destroying you, even if it once called you "family."

Let Go of the Past, Step Into the Now

Too often, we get stuck in what was and miss what is. We replay old mistakes like broken records. Cling to grudges like trophies. Compare the present to a past we've polished and glorified. But living in there is like trying to drive forward while staring only in the rearview mirror. Eventually, you crash or, worse, you stay stuck.

Yet it's feels safe and familiar. Even when it hurts, at least you know the story. But here's the truth: you can't change it. No amount of replaying, rethinking, or regret will rewrite it. The only thing that can change is you. And that change only happens now.

When you live in the past, you disconnect from what's real. You miss the people trying to love you now. The growth is happening inside you now. The moments are already carrying healing.

Letting go doesn't mean erasing what happened.
It means refusing to let it define what comes next.
Your story didn't end. It paused. And now, you get to turn the page.

You might not have a clear path. You might feel unsure. But staying stuck doesn't protect you. It shrinks you. The world gets smaller. You get smaller.
And the life you deserve slips further away.

So move forward, even if your steps are shaky, and the future feels like a blur. You don't need all the answers at once. Just go. One step. Then another. No matter how uncertain or how hard it feels.

Each step you take is a win. You kept going, even when everything inside you said to stop. That's not just healing. That's leaving the past where it belongs and stepping into a life that's still yours.

I Don't Hold Grudges
I Remember

Let me be clear. I don't hold grudges.
Holding a grudge means carrying anger and bitterness, and that's not my path.

What I carry are the facts. Plain and simple.
The things that happened, the choices that were made, the words that were spoken.
I hold these facts not to punish or hurt, but to acknowledge what truly happened.
The unfiltered truth, without excuses or distortions.
These facts remind me of the reality I lived, helping me guard my peace and protect my heart.

I refuse to carry shame, guilt, or blame that aren't mine to bear.

I return to you full responsibility and ownership of those terrible things.
They were your choices, not mine.
I did not do those things, and I never will.
I let that burden stay where it belongs, with you.
This is me setting myself free, letting you hold what you created. It isn't about revenge or anger. It's me saying I refuse to let your mistakes define or weigh me down.
That part of the story ends here.

When You Finally See Who They Truly Are

When you finally see who they truly are, a broken, unhealed person carrying wounds that have never fully healed, it changes everything. You realize they are intensely afraid of their own emotions, almost as if those feelings scare them more than anything else.

They don't know how to face those feelings, so they try to bury or ignore them. At the same time, they feel deeply uncomfortable with themselves, as if there's a part inside that they don't like or don't know how to accept. This discomfort makes them restless and sometimes pushes them to act in ways that seem confusing or hurtful.

Once you see this, you begin to understand their actions, the way they react, the things they say, or the walls they put up around themselves. Their behavior isn't about you; it's about their own struggle, fear, and pain. They might lash out or shut down, not out of choice but from not knowing any better.

Recognizing this doesn't excuse the pain they cause, but it helps you feel empathy instead of anger or frustration. You see that behind those actions is a person who is deeply struggling, and that understanding changes how you relate to them and maybe even how you see yourself.

Living with the Pain

There's no magic fix for betrayal. No switch you can flip to make the pain vanish. At first, it feels overwhelming, like it's going to swallow you whole. You wake up with it pressing on your chest. It's the first thing you think about. Nights aren't much better. Sleep offers no relief, just restlessness, maybe even nightmares.

But then, slowly and almost without you realizing it, it shifts. The pain doesn't disappear, but you begin to carry it differently. It becomes part of your story, not the whole thing. One day, you wake up and it's still there, but it's no longer the first thing on your mind. Maybe it's second. Maybe third. That small breath of distance, that sliver of space, is how healing begins.

Healing doesn't mean pretending it didn't happen or forcing yourself to feel "okay." It means moving forward, even when the pain tags along. That's real strength, not in erasing the hurt, but in learning to live beside it, one day at a time.

A New Chance

One of the most comforting things about life is this: every single day, you're given a new beginning. An honest chance to start over, not by becoming someone completely different, but by stepping forward as a softer, stronger, wiser version of who you already are.

It doesn't matter how messy yesterday was. Maybe it left you drained. Maybe you made mistakes. Maybe it all blurred together in a cycle of stress and routine. Or maybe it was filled with laughter, growth, or hard-won peace. Either way, today has arrived. A blank page. An invitation to begin again, with a little more grace, a little more clarity, and a little more kindness toward yourself.

You are not tied to your past. You are not trapped in old versions of yourself. You are allowed to outgrow the things that once defined you. You are allowed to pause, to reflect, to breathe, and to shift directions slowly and gently.

Growth doesn't always look big or loud. Sometimes it's found in the way you speak to yourself when no one's listening, in the way you choose understanding over self-judgment, in the courage it takes to keep going even when you don't have it all figured out.

And sometimes the most powerful transformation doesn't start with a grand moment or a dramatic shift. It begins with a single deep breath, a small act of self-care, or the decision to simply show up for yourself again, exactly as you are, and try.

That is what a new chance really is. Not pressure to become perfect, but the freedom to become real.

Despite the Storm

Nobody hands you a guidebook for life. One minute you're just trying to make coffee, and the next the whole sky decides to drop on your head. No announcements. No invitations. Just a full-blown emotional thunderstorm landing right in your lap. Suddenly, getting out of bed feels like you're training for a marathon, and breathing deserves its own trophy.

No one warns you that life will throw you into the deep end without so much as a floatie. You didn't get a coat. You didn't get directions. Just vibes, disappointment and a vague sense of what even is this.

And yet, you didn't disappear into a puddle of self-pity. You didn't glide through it like some spiritually enlightened yoga instructor. You tripped. You sobbed in weird places. You rage-cleaned your apartment at midnight. But you kept moving anyway.

You've swallowed heartache like it was part of your breakfast. Stumbled through days that felt like a group project where everyone bailed, and you were stuck doing the emotional heavy lifting. It was messy. It was lonely. And you're still here.

That's not nothing. In fact, it's everything.

You could have checked out. You didn't. You stayed. You took the leftovers of your worst days and made something. Maybe not polished. Maybe not symmetrical. But something solid. Something that holds.

So, if today feels like another round of emotional dodgeball, just remember you've made it through every single mess so far. That's not luck. That's resilience. Or stubbornness. Or maybe both. Either way, it's working.

And that is honestly kind of legendary.

The Breakup That Broke You to Save You

A breakup isn't just a split. It's a war you never signed up for but still had to fight. It's not just the end of a relationship, but the death of a beautiful lie. A lie that once made you feel chosen, seen, like you finally found what you were always waiting for.

Only to discover it was never love. It was a game. He lifted you high just to drop you hard, watching you break and search for him in every dark corner like he was your only way out. One day, he adored you. The next, you were invisible. He made you feel like the most wanted person in the world, then turned around and made you feel like nothing.

He whispered "I love you" with the same mouth he used to kiss someone else. And while you sat there blaming yourself, trying to figure out what you did wrong, you missed the truth: he never loved you, **not 'cause you weren't worthy. He just never saw love as something reserved only for you.**

To him, you weren't a person. You were a source of attention, admiration, and control. And now that you're gone, he misses the power, not the love. He wants you back, not since he sees your worth, but as he's losing the grip he once had on you.

But here's the thing. Leaving isn't the hardest part. Not going back is. And one day, he'll come knocking again. Calling you "the one that got away." Saying he was lost, that no one compares. And maybe a part of you will want to believe it.

The real breakup doesn't happen when you walk away. It happens when you realize there's nothing left to go back to and you stop hoping, waiting, or needing any kind of closure.

It happens when you start putting yourself back together, piece by piece. That's when its hits you, you're finally free.

The Only Place I See You Now

You came to me in my dream last night, and for a little while, it felt like nothing had changed, like you were still here, and never left. We talked the way we always used to. You hugged me, and it felt so real, I didn't want to wake up.
For the first time in what feels like forever, my heart didn't feel so empty.

But then I opened my eyes, and the moment was gone.
The pain of losing you hit me all over again, just like it did the first time.

I lay there, not moving, staring at the ceiling, trying to breathe through the weight in my chest and deep down, I know I'll never see you again, not really. Only in heaven.

But for now, if dreams are the only place I can find you, then I'll take them. I'll take every heartbreaking second. I'll take the emptiness that follows when I wake up.

And for those few moments...you were real again. And that's all I have left.

With love,
Bella.

You Might Be the Villain, and That's Okay

At some point, you'll be the villain in someone else's story. That's just how it goes. The version told won't look anything like what actually happened. But it'll stick. That version makes it easier to move on for them. That person won't mention how many times you kept things to yourself to keep the peace. Or how often you sat with the truth, unsure what to do with it. There won't be any talk about how much it took just to stay present when nothing was getting through.

You'll be described in simple terms. Distant. Uncaring. Abrupt. As if it all ended in one moment instead of unraveling over time. It'll sound neat. Digestible. Easy to pass along.

People like their stories clean. No loose ends. No shared responsibility.

Don't chase it. Don't correct every version floating around. The truth lives in you, not in the words being passed between others.

Let them have their story if it helps them sleep. You don't need to hold it for them anymore.

You know what you carried what really happened and what was asked of you, and how much of yourself got lost in the process. You walked away, not out of spite, but from something finished. There was nothing left to repair. No more pieces to gather or waiting for someone to finally see what it cost you to stay.

You're not the villain. You just knew it was already over. They never change. And maybe that's as close as it gets for now. Some endings don't need closure. They need distance, silence, and the strength to live with being misunderstood by the people you once would've broken yourself to be understood by. That's the part no one sees, and no one ever asks about.

Some Doors Should Stay Closed

When someone shows up acting different doesn't mean they've changed in the ways that matter. People can learn new words without changing their intentions. It's easy to copy what healing sounds like. It's something else to live in a way that proves it. Someone who once tried to tear you down, your name, your peace, your relationships, should never be handed an easy return. That kind of harm isn't erased by silence or soft looks. It stays. It remembers. And the ones who caused it often hope you won't.

A snake doesn't stop being a snake just **'cause it's low this time.** Sometimes the most dangerous people come back wearing calm like a disguise. They know how to wait. They know how to look harmless. But there's something cold underneath. Something that didn't go anywhere.

Growth isn't proven through apologies. It's shown in changed behavior when there's nothing to gain. Not when eyes are on them. Not when forgiveness is expected. The truth shows up in what they do when you're no longer within reach. Protect your peace and your progress. You've come too far, hurt too much, lost more than anyone knows. What you've built didn't appear out of nowhere. It was earned. Day by day. Alone, if we're being honest.

Not everyone deserves a second chance at the version of you that had to rebuild. That version cost you everything. It was built from damage they caused.

The Deepest Scars

Most pain fades with time. Life knocks us down, yet somehow we get back up. We move forward with the help of time, resilience, and the right people by our side.

But the hurt caused by someone we trusted is a different kind of pain. The kind that doesn't just bruise your heart but shakes your foundation. You let them in, believed in them, and they left you with wounds no one can see, but you still feel.

That kind of damage lingers. It changes the way you see people, the way you protect yourself, and the way you love.

And healing isn't off the table. It's slow. It's messy. Some days it feels like you're getting nowhere then little by little, things shift.

One day you'll look back and realize the scar is still there, but it doesn't hurt like it used to. And maybe it even reminds you of your strength. Not of what happened, but of what you made it through.

Hands That Didn't Let Go
(Reflective Prose)

He ran his hands over my past.

Lingering over the dents and the deeply worn edges of my heart. I was looking at him, and when I thought *he wouldn't stay after finding out how broken I was,* he sat me down and told me I was a warrior, and that I'd never have to fight another battle alone.

He made me understand trauma isn't just what happened to me; it's what didn't happen. It's the care I didn't receive. The protection I wasn't given when I needed it the most.

He said:
I know this transformation is painful, but you're not falling apart; you're just falling into something different, with a new capacity to be wiser. I'll be your home. Your peace, or your shield if you need it, cause you are already dealing with your demons.
And though that road is one you must walk alone, I'll always be near, close enough to hold your hand if you get scared in the dark.

With love,
Bella.

The Kind of Tired No One Sees

No one talks about the kind of tired that sleep can't fix. The kind that settles under your skin. That turns your mood into a broken switch, flipping between "I'm okay," "I don't care," and "I don't know how much longer I can keep this up."

Sometimes, it flips so fast you can't even catch it. One minute you're smiling in a room full of people, five minutes later you're staring at your phone, wondering what the point of any of it even is.

You tell yourself it's just a bad day. Then it's a bad week.

Eventually, you stop counting. It's too much to keep track of when you don't care anymore.

You move through the motions: eat, shower, work, respond. But it's all fog…like watching someone else live your life while you're trapped behind glass.

And the worst part? No one sees it. You've worn "I'm fine" so long it fits like armor, laugh at the right times. Text back. Show up.
But you're not really there.

Some nights, your heart races, thoughts too loud to sleep. But in the morning, you get up anyway. Not out of strength. Not hope. Just reflex. Something survival taught you.

And still, no one says, I see you unraveling, and that smile is a shield. They just say, "You've changed," like you chose to become a ghost of yourself. But you didn't. You're just tired of trying. And stuck in a body that knows how to fake being okay
while your mind quietly whispers,

"I don't know how much longer I can do this."

Some Days You Miss the Pain

It sounds strange, maybe even wrong, but it's true. When pain has been your constant companion, it becomes familiar. Like an old sweater you never liked but wore anyway, you just knew how it fit. You don't want to suffer. You don't believe pain is good.
But when everything else feels uncertain, pain feels solid. Something you understand. When you've carried hurt for years, it settles deep.

It lives in your bones, your breath, the way you move through the world. You grow used to the weight of it, pressing down, a dull gravity you learned to live under. And even when it begins to lift, when light starts to slip through the cracks, there's grief. A strange mourning for what nearly broke you. For so long, it was part of you.
And without it?

You're not always sure who you are. If the pain is gone, what's left in its place? Not peace, at least not yet. Just silence. And sometimes, the silence is louder than the hurt ever was. You catch yourself reaching back. Not to relive it, but to remember it. At least the pain was real. You knew what it was. You knew who you were in it.

Missing the pain doesn't mean you want it back. It means you're grieving the only thing that ever felt consistent. A twisted kind of friend, unwanted but reliable.

And some days, the ache you feel isn't the pain itself, it's the absence of it. The emptiness it left behind.

But even that longing means something has shifted.

It means you're beginning to move, and there's space inside you that pain no longer owns. And maybe, with time, that space will be filled with something else, something softer. Something kind.

So yes, it's okay to miss the pain. To grieve it. Healing is never clean. It stumbles. It scars. It tears. But even the sadness means you're on your way.

Cost of Comfort

You spent your whole life making sure everyone else felt at ease, only to wake up one day and realize you never did.

It wasn't on purpose. It began with little things: softening your tone, laughing at jokes that didn't land, swallowing your truth to keep the peace. You told yourself it was kindness. Maturity. Compassion. You believed being easy to be around made you better.

But slowly, without even noticing, you began to disappear.
You held space for everyone else's feelings while burying your own. You became the steady one, the quiet anchor, the person others turned to when their worlds were unraveling. And somewhere in the process, you lost track of yourself.

Now you look around at the life you've built, a life where everyone else can breathe freely.

Except you.

You were the comfort. But you never got to feel it.

He Called It Love

He called it love.
But for you, it was survival.

It wasn't the kind of love that makes your chest rise with hope or your heart race with possibility. It was the kind that made you hold your breath, bracing for the next hurt, the next silence, the next moment you'd question if you were enough. A love that demanded everything but returned so little. One that felt safe. Not from healing, but from how well you protected yourself inside it.

You grasped at the safe fragments like a lifeline, the rare moments when he wasn't angry or distant, when his touch didn't sting and his words didn't wound. You called those moments love just to have something steady, something to hold on to. But deep down, you knew it was something else. Something that masked its pain with promises and devotion, never fully revealing what lurked beneath.

This love was endurance. Carrying the weight of silent apologies and broken vows. Waking each day wondering if this time it might change, and falling asleep knowing it probably wouldn't. Learning to read between the lines, finding meaning in the unsaid, gripping on tight even when your fingers bled.

The nights you longed to escape. The days you wore a smile like armor. The moments you convinced yourself that pain was just another name for love. Sometimes love isn't warmth or light. It's the fire you walk through, the storm you endure, the quiet battle no one else sees.

Maybe that's what he meant by love.
But for you, love wasn't just love.
It was survival.

The Bitter Truth About Ignored Warnings and Broken Trust

The early signs: the broken promises, the self-centeredness, the quiet disregard for your boundaries, aren't harmless quirks. They're warnings. Subtle at first, then louder, until they echo like sirens. But you silence them. You tell yourself they'll change...that things will get better. That love, patience, or understanding might fix what's clearly fractured.

But here is the bitter truth: some people never change. They don't grow. They don't reflect or heal. No matter how much space you give them to rise, they choose to stay the same, caught in their own dysfunction, unwilling to confront what needs to shift. And if you stay, they will take you down with them.

That uneasy feeling you get? Trust it. It's not paranoia. It's perception. When someone reveals who they are through actions soaked in cruelty, manipulation, or indifference, believe it. Don't wait for it to escalate into something you can't ignore. Pain shouldn't be the proof.

You don't need to be the one who saves them. You're not responsible for their healing. You never were. The bravest thing you can do is walk away the moment someone shows you they are not willing to meet you with the same care you offer. Protect your peace. Guard it like your life depends on it, and sometimes, emotionally, it does.

The Emptiness Inside You No One Sees
(not that you ask, but here it is.)

You smile when people look. That kind of practiced one that doesn't show in the eyes, only the mouth. The sort people accept without asking anything. It gets easier with time. That surface version of you. Chatting, nodding, laughing at the right moments. Holding a coffee cup like everything is fine, standing in rooms like you belong there, but you don't, not anymore and you know it. Answering messages like your heart isn't pulled out and left somewhere else.

Inside, it feels like something has gone missing. Just... gone. Like a room you visit has been emptied overnight. And no one else can see it. You never mention the name anymore. Not out loud. Not even in passing. That makes it real, and real means you still care. And you already tell yourself you don't.

You act like nothing touches you anymore. Like you finally figure out how to move on. The kind of moving on that's all show, hair brushed, errands done, showing up to things with clean clothes and dry eyes. No one asks the hard questions, so you don't have to lie. Just let them believe what they want to. Let them think time heals something.
But every night when the noise dies down, it hits you again. That stretch of silence where that person lives. The part where a call comes in, or a message, or a face at the door. And now there's nothing. Just air. Just the same goddamn songs on the radio, the same roads with too many turns, the feeling that none of it fits right anymore.
But no matter how well you pretend, or how hard you try to replace them, you know you'll never be whole without that person.

So you keep telling yourself it is pride, but deep down it is more than that. It is fear. Fear that if you ever reach out, no one will be there. Or worse, someone will answer, and you will fold. So you keep your head up and your mouth shut. Make jokes. Change the subject. Pour more beer. Switch the lights off early and pretend the tiredness is physical.

Every day feels like holding your breath underwater. Long enough that maybe people think you are floating. But you know the truth. You know what you did. That's why you're stuck in that empty room, pretending you left it behind. But one person always knew. And the worst part? You see them in everything. And act like you don't.

Not Every Memory Deserves a Place in Your Heart

Not every moment is worth keeping. We don't like to admit that. We've been told our entire lives that everything happens for a reason, that every second counts, that every experience somehow shapes us.

But the truth is, some pieces of the past do nothing but weigh us down and pull us backwards. Some stay with us not for their value or meaning, but simply for how much they hurt. They replay in our heads late at night, whispering things we wish we could forget—things we said in regret, things they did to us, things we didn't deserve.

And somehow, over time, we let them shape who we become, even though not every part of the past is worth holding on to. Still, we carry them. We think we're supposed to. The world tells us that letting go is the same as giving up or pretending it never happened.

Letting go doesn't mean it didn't matter. It means it no longer gets to define us.

It means it no longer gets to control our emotions, our peace, or our future.

When Silence Became Strength

I knew I had matured, not just aged, but truly grown when I chose silence instead of tearing down people I could have easily exposed. Not doe to the fact they didn't deserve it. Maybe they did. But I couldn't bring myself to go where they had gone. It wasn't that I lacked the words or the chance. I held both, along with the receipts, and they would have hit hard.

And let's be honest, when you're hurt or angry, there is a certain satisfaction in making someone feel what they made you feel. Revenge can look like justice when your heart is still healing. And yes, a younger version of me might have done it. Quick. Sharp. Unforgiving.

But this time, something in me paused. I looked at the situation and at them, not through the lens of what they deserved, but through the person I wanted to be. And I realized I don't want to be them. Maturity is knowing it's not about winning anymore. It's about choosing not to use your power just to feed your ego. Walking away with your peace instead of the broken pride. Not from weakness, but from knowing the cost of causing pain. And your peace matters more than making a point.

Some people will never apologize. They will never admit what they did. They may never change. And that's okay. Your healing isn't tied to their remorse. It's your decision to move forward without needing revenge.

So yes, I could have brought them down. Worse than what they did to me. Yet I walked away with my dignity intact, but most importantly with my hands clean.

Your Spark Finally Decides to Show Up Again

So, guess who finally decided to return from their extended vacation? That little thing called your spark, not with a bang, of course. That would be far too helpful.

No, it creeps in like it never ghosted you in the first place. One minute you're lying on the floor contemplating the meaning of laundry, and the next, you're updating your to-do list like you have your life together.

You start doing things. Real, productive things. Like replying to emails you ignored three weeks ago. Or suddenly feeling inspired to clean the kitchen just like that.

Creative ideas? Flowing.
Sense of purpose? Tentatively peeking through.

So, my lovely, when your spark returns, don't ask where it's been. Just roll your eyes, make a coffee, and get back to being mildly impressive.

Loving Someone Who Looks Outward
To Feel Worthy Can Leave You Feeling Invisible

When your partner constantly seeks validation from others, it can feel confusing, painful, and even threatening. You might find yourself wondering, "Am I not enough?" or "Why isn't my love enough for them to feel secure?" But the truth is, their need for external validation often speaks more to their inner wounds than to your relationship's value.

People who crave validation from others may be struggling with deep-rooted insecurities, wounds that existed long before you came into their life. Maybe they never felt truly seen, appreciated, or loved for who they are.

Maybe somewhere along the way, they learned that their worth depended on how others responded to them. And while understanding this can help soften the sting, it doesn't make it easy.

You deserve a partner who feels safe and whole with you, someone who doesn't need applause from the world to feel significant. Love isn't a stage, and it's not something that needs to be put on display to be real.

If you're in this situation, it's okay to voice your feelings. You are allowed to say "It hurts when it feels like being seen by others matters more to you than being here with me." you're allowed to protect your peace and draw the lines you need.

And if they're open , care enough to listen, remind them gently: the kind of validation that truly heals doesn't come from strangers. It comes from within and from someone who loves you even when no one's watching.

Betrayal Reflections

The door creaked open quietly as I stepped into the room, expecting nothing more than a casual gathering of friends. But what I walked into stopped me cold. Laughter filled the air, sharp, familiar voices but the words they spoke weren't meant for me to hear. They were talking about me. About my relationship with someone. Harsh words, ridicule disguised as humor, critiques cloaked in mock concern. My heart sank. They didn't know I was there.

I stood for a moment, unseen in the doorway, my presence veiled by their own indifference. As their words settled in my chest like stones, I didn't say a word. I simply shook my head, a bitter smile forming on my lips. Then slowly I turned and walked away, leaving behind not just the room but the illusion of friendship I once held dear.

But that wasn't the only betrayal I endured.
There was once someone I called my friend. The kind of friend you share every piece of your life with. We laughed until we cried, whispered secrets under the stars, and leaned on each other in life's darkest moments. I believed we were inseparable. Unbreakable. Until the day I discovered the truth.

What they did behind my back wasn't just disloyal. It was something unimaginable. Something so deep, it stole the breath from my lungs. When I found out, it wasn't just the act itself that hurt. It was the realization that the person I trusted most had harbored such deceit. The wound cut deeper it came from the one place I thought was safe.

That pain changed me. It taught me that sometimes, the people closest to you can cause the greatest harm. That smiles can be masks, and loyalty can be a lie.
But it also taught me something powerful.

I learned the strength in silence. The wisdom in walking away. I began to see people more clearly, not for the words they speak, but the truths their actions reveal. And most of all, I learned to treasure the rare souls who remain steadfast, even when the skies turn gray. Those are the ones worth keeping. The ones who never need to be watched to be trusted.

Give, But Don't Be Taken for Granted

Generosity, loyalty, and kindness are beautiful qualities. They show strength, not weakness. Being someone who gives without expecting anything in return, who sticks by the people they care about, and who treats others with warmth and compassion is something rare and valuable in this world. But here is the thing: those qualities only shine when they are given to the right people.

You can pour your heart into someone, be there for them time and time again, and still end up feeling unappreciated or even used. Not everyone will value your kindness. Some will come to expect it, even demand it, without ever giving anything back. The more you give, the less they seem to care, as if your efforts mean less simply as they are always there. That is when it hurts the most. Not that you expect a reward, but it feels like your love, effort, and loyalty are invisible.

That is why it is so important to set boundaries. Not walls. Walls shut everyone out, even the people who deserve a place in your life. Boundaries are different. They protect your energy. They help you recognize when enough is enough, when to stop giving, and when to walk away. Boundaries say, "I love you, but I love myself too."

Loyalty is a gift, not a guarantee. It should never be one-sided. If someone cannot see the value in your loyalty, if they take it for granted, they will likely only realize its worth once it is gone. And by then, it might be too late.

So, be generous. Be loyal. Be kind. But be smart about who you give those parts of yourself to. You deserve relationships that feel mutual, where your heart is not just open but also safe.

The Language of Small Things.
Even on the Hardest Days

The Last Language of a Fading Life

Even on days when he was too sick to speak, when lifting his head felt like moving mountains, he still found a way. The words would abandon him first, slipping through the cracks of a weary mind and a trembling mouth. His hands, once steady and strong, now betrayed him with shakes that rattled cups and thoughts alike.

And somehow, despite it all, he never failed to make her coffee. He knew just how she liked it. Not too hot, black with sugar. It wasn't grand. It wasn't diamonds or dramatic gestures.

It was coffee in bed. Simply.

Yet, every morning, without fail, she'd smiled like it was the first time. To her, it wasn't just a drink.

It was proof that someone had thought of her the moment they woke up. Love, brewed and served in silence, with sugar and care.

It became his language when words were gone. A ritual carved into the silence. The click of the kettle. The rustle of the tin. The warm, familiar aroma that filled the kitchen. These were his I love yous.

Some days, she'd try to stop him, whispering soft protests he'd ignore with a weak but determined smile.

Other times, she only watched from the doorway, arms folded, heart aching, memorizing the shape of his love and fearing the day it might stop. He poured more love into a mug than most could speak in a lifetime.

She knew. For him, it wasn't about the coffee. It never was.

It was the last thing he could do for her without help, the last piece of normal he could offer in a life slowly being rewritten by illness. And so, every morning, even when it took everything he had, he showed up for her. One small cup at a time.

With love. As always.
Bella.

Words and Pictures
Truths We Can't Escape

I love words, both the ones I write myself and those that seem to find me just when I need them most. There's something about language that can hold you up or break you down, sometimes in the same breath.

Words carry weight, power, and sometimes a sharp edge you don't see coming until it cuts deep.

And then there are pictures. I love them too, the ones I capture with my own eyes and the ones others send me, like secret windows into moments I wasn't meant to witness. Pictures don't just show you what's in front of you; they pull back the curtain on what's happening behind your back. They reveal the real world in ways words often fail to. Unfiltered, raw, and loud.

Like people, pictures talk. They tell stories of beauty and decay, of love and betrayal, of hope and lies. They freeze moments in time that are often too honest to ignore. And that honesty is dangerous.

Sometimes, pictures catch things you wish you never saw, not due to the pain being new, but as the disappointment stings all over again. The frustration with people who stoop lower than you thought possible, all in the name of just to have it, whatever "it" means to them.

It's a shame, really. How low some people can go, how far they can fall, all while pretending to be something better.

And yet, here we are, living in this tangled mess of words and images, forced to confront truths we'd rather bury. And the hardest part isn't what we see or hear. It's realizing how much of it we once refused to believe.

Yet, in the end, the real betrayal isn't what the pictures show but what we let ourselves ignore.

You Showed Me Safe Again

You found me when I was broken.

Not just shattered and lost, but sinking, silent, unseen. And you didn't try to fix me. You sat with me in the dark, patiently, and teaching me that time was not my enemy. It was only a healer.

Your soul... God, your soul.
It was soft where the world had grown sharp. Your touch, your voice, they didn't just soothe. They reminded me of what being safe felt like. There was a purity in you, a rare kind of gentleness that didn't ask for attention. It just was. Like breath. Like light.

I knew then, you weren't just special.
You were sacred. You didn't heal what you broke. You healed what others shattered in me. You poured love into the cracks without ever asking why they were there.

You gave me everything without needing a single thing in return. And that... that is why there is no one like you. Not even close.

Maybe that's why the angels called you home too early, as if even heaven couldn't bear the distance from a soul like yours.

With love,
Bella.

Why I Sometimes Disappear

I need people to understand something: I can't be there for them all the time. Not that I don't care or I don't want to. But sometimes I'm sinking too.

I've learned how to wear a steady face. How to pretend like I have it together. But underneath, I'm just trying to stay afloat. Most days, survival feels like an invisible job.

There are nights I just climb into bed, broken, shaking, staring out of my window and asking the same quiet question over and over: "What now?"

So no, I can't always be the strong one. I can't always hold space for others. Truthfully, there are moments I can't even hold space for myself.

And that's why, however selfish it may seem, my heart holds tightly to the people who show up for me. The ones who didn't give up on me. Who just come to check if I'm OK and offer help without expecting anything in return.

The ones who sense the storm in me without needing it explained, and choose to stay with me anyway. That kind of love...it's rare. And when I receive it, I feel seen. I feel less alone. I feel human again.

Someday, when I've found steadier ground, when the waves inside me settle, I want to give that love back. I want to be that safe place for someone else.

But until then, I'll keep fighting. For better days. For breath. For the chance to become what others have been for me.

Borrowed Spark

I haven't lost my spark. It just isn't with me right now.
Someone borrowed it, maybe a few people did for a while, maybe without even meaning to. I gave it away, piece by piece, thinking I could spare it.

You know how it goes. It wasn't dramatic. No big moment, no final straw. Just little things: listening when I had nothing left to give, when I was the one who needed to be heard. Smiling when I wanted to cry.
Saying "I'm fine" when I wasn't even close.

You try to be the strong one, the steady one,
until one day you look in the mirror and don't even recognize the tired eyes staring back.
So you just stand there and think: I thought if I was useful, if I was kind, if I kept showing up, I'd feel like myself again. But the reality is, I've been running on empty for longer than I want to admit.

And now, there are days I wake up and wonder where I went. Not just the energy or the laughter, but the part of me that used to feel alive. It's not that I'm broken. Just... dimmed. Like a candle still burning, but quieter now, softer.

Some days I really miss her, the version of me who didn't feel so heavy, so invisible, so forgotten by her own heart. But for now, I'll just sit here alone and hope my spark remembers the way home.

I didn't lose her. She's just out there somewhere, with the people and pieces of me I handed out on days I forgot to save any for myself.

But I'll get it back, one morning, one moment, one deep breath at a time.

The Drawer
(Fragments Of A Life)

There were nights the hunger made her hallucinate. Not dreams or wishes. Just crawling thoughts that came when her stomach had nothing left to burn. She counted the cracks in the ceiling to keep herself from slipping under. One hundred twelve. Over and over, even after they vanished behind smoke, plaster, or fists.

He never hit her the same way twice. Sometimes it was his hand. Sometimes the belt or whatever he grabbed on his way through to her. His words slurred and tangled, rarely making sense. But his hands never missed. Some nights he didn't bother with his hands at all. He kicked her until she bled. Until her body curled in on itself and didn't move. Dodging made it worse, so she stopped trying.

She was six the first time. The milk slipped. It wasn't on purpose. The bottle cracked across the floor and soaked into the mat by the door. He didn't ask. Didn't look. Just stepped through the mess and swung. What stayed wasn't the fall, but the sound it made when it struck her ribs.

After that, the rules changed. Don't speak unless asked. Don't eat unless it's offered. Don't cry where he can see. If there was food on the stove, wait. Sometimes he skipped the meal just to make her wait longer.

Hunger drove her to the stores. She took what she could. The workers, when they saw her come in, just disappeared and let it happen. No one stopped her. They saw enough to understand, and that was the choice they made for her.

That kind of mercy stayed longer than food ever did. She knew stealing was wrong, but there wasn't another way.

By then, even her shame had learned how to stay still.

Movement became silent. Breathing turned careful. Some nights, she hid under the bed and stayed there until her body stopped shaking.

But no matter how much he hurt her, she didn't break. With a broken voice, when her body couldn't even stand straight, she said it. Over and over:

"You can't hurt me. You're not my father."

That's what made him keep going. He didn't want bruises. He wanted her soul to split. And when it didn't, he came back harder.

He saw something he couldn't name. Starved. Crawling. Still, there was a way she carried herself, like something inside hadn't died yet. That made him furious. She wasn't supposed to have anything. Not pride, dignity or defiance. But it was there, and he hated her for it.

He beat to kill that part. Not the girl. What she held inside.

One Christmas, he left a knife on the table. No wrapping. No name. No explanation. He didn't need one. After that, he only had to raise his voice and glance toward the drawer. That was enough.

That winter, growth halted. Clothes no longer fit. Hair thinned. Teachers noticed. They asked questions. She lied. Said it happened on a swing that didn't exist.

No one followed up. No call. No knock. Nothing.

He didn't quit until she was nearly grown. By then, there was nothing left for him to reach. When he shouted, her body didn't flinch. Her mind had gone somewhere else. Still cleaned. Still moved through rooms. But she'd already left. Slipped out years before.

One day, something deep in her chest gave out. Not from him. Not from hunger. Something smaller. And it never came back. Yet finally found a way to run and never return.

They called her lucky. Said she got out. That she lived. As if watching counted. Like doing nothing to save a child meant they deserved a piece of her crawl out.

True Meaning of Courage

Sometimes, we smile even when we're broken inside. We laugh through the silence, masking the pain that no one sees. For a long time, I believed that hiding our struggles was a sign of bravery, that keeping everything inside made us strong.

But I've come to realize that true courage isn't about hiding our pain. True courage is showing the world our tears, our fears, and still standing tall despite it all. It's allowing ourselves to be vulnerable and real, even when it feels hard.

And in that honesty, in that openness, we find a strength that can't be hidden. That strength, that is what truly defines bravery.

A long time ago, someone very special to my heart told me something I'll never forget.

He said,
"You have the power to turn people into poetry, Bella, your tears are beautiful words, and they need to be written."

He was right.
He saw me, truly saw me, when no one else even looked. He understood what writing meant to me: that it was life itself. Writing was the only thing that could pull me from that dark, cold place where even breathing felt like breaking.
He knew me better than anyone else ever had.

He believed in me when I couldn't believe in myself. And somehow, that belief lit a fire in the darkness. It gave me courage to face the pain, to tell my story. Bleed ink and call it healing. For me that was the only way to survive my ache.

And I want to remind all of you today: it's okay to be vulnerable. It's okay to show your scars. Cause in those moments of honesty that we can find our greatest strength, to create something real.

Love,
Bella.

Whispered in the Winds, Remembered in the Soul

You left, but your love remains.

That feeling when you have to take the first breath after he has just taken his last in your arms. Waking up the next morning and realizing it wasn't a nightmare. He really wasn't coming back. Stepping outside the house for the first time, everything feels different, hollow.

When people ask you, "Where is he?" and you have to say, "He's gone." And the words feel like glass in your throat. It changes you forever.

I would trade it all.
I'd give up everything I own if I could turn the clock back to a time before the angels called you home. I wish there had been more I could do. I should have held you stronger that night, when you whispered all you felt inside before you took your last breath.
Just one more hug. A little moment longer...

I still miss the sound of your voice, the wisdom of your advice, the stories you told. And everything changed the moment you left.
It feels like time just keeps moving without me. But the truth is, the grief never left me. Forever, I will mourn.

I know it's been years since you've gone, yet some days it still hits me like a train. Like it just happened. It sits with me. And I still don't know how to live with it. Some days, still turn into anger. It presses down on my chest until it feels like too much. But even then, I know it's grief's way of reminding me I was truly blessed.

But selfishly, right now, I need you more than ever.

As always,
With love,
Bella.

When You Left, My World Fell Silent

I was hugging you in our bed and I couldn't move, I couldn't let you go... I was paralyzed to the spot. I wanted to make a sound, but nothing came out. Nothing happened when I opened my mouth. That moment hit me with this pain in my heart that went through to my soul. It was a pain I had never felt before. It was excruciating. I refused to believe it. I couldn't believe it.

How?
How could you go? How could you leave me alone here, in this cold, cruel world? Why can't you take me with you, please, I beg you to come back, and take me too.

After what felt like an eternity, there was a sound, a terrible, gut-wrenching scream followed by the deepest sobs I ever heard. And suddenly I realized that when people were looking at me, I was the one who was making these heartbreaking sounds that I didn't even know would be possible to make. And The moment you closed your eyes forever, my whole world collapsed.

And I am so lost without you.

With love,
Bella.

The Shift That Changed Me:
Breaking, Healing, Becoming
(Personal Reflection)

My life had fallen apart, but somehow, it fell back together at the same time.
Not through some grand revelation or feel-good turning point. Just slowly, unevenly, in ways that only make sense when I look back now.

Every person who let me go, or who I let go, every so-called friend who drifted away when my life got too messy, too heavy, was replaced by something better.
Not perfect people, but real ones. The kind who show up without needing a spotlight. Who stay even when I have nothing to offer but tears, misery, and mess, and I'll be there for them too, a million times over if they need me.

I used to mourn the ones who left. Wondered if I'd been softer, less of a drama, or if I'd faked my happiness and hidden my pain when I was around them, they might have stayed.
At the same time, I had to admit I wasn't without fault. I have my share in the story, too. But now I understand: some people are chapters, not constants. And trying to keep them in your story only stops you from turning the page. But still, there were nights I couldn't sleep, heavy with questions that never got answers. Mornings, I woke up already tired from carrying too much silence. I smiled when I didn't mean it. Said I was fine when I wasn't even close. I wasn't just exhausted. I was done. Broken.

Yet life didn't stop. And somehow, neither did I.

It wasn't brave or graceful. But I kept moving. And somewhere along the way, I stopped begging for things to go back to how they were. I stopped explaining myself to people committed to misunderstanding me.

So I let go. Slowly, uneasily, but I let go.

And in that space, something new began. I started showing up for myself. I stopped chasing or thinking about people who caused me pain. I started choosing what felt honest, even when it didn't feel easy.

That's when I finally realized, maybe strength isn't about always staying unbroken, it's about how many times you rebuild. Maybe it's not about confidence, but consistency, the kind that keeps showing up even with shaking hands.

Now, when something ends, when people walk away, or I need to, I still feel it. But I don't unravel like I used to. I know now that not everything that breaks is a loss. Some things fall apart just to make space for what's real to finally arrive.

What Grief Left Behind
(Dissociative Self-Reflection)

"They said she vanished, you know?
Just disappeared. One day she was there, and then... gone."

But that's not the truth.
Not really.

She didn't vanish.
Grief found her. And it didn't come crashing in like a storm. It came slowly, like a fog. It crept into her bones before anyone noticed, sat heavy in her chest, and stayed. It wasn't loud or scream. It just settled there, heavy and invisible. She still laughed at the right moments, showed up when she was supposed to, wore the same clothes and said the same things. But she was slipping. Fading in small pieces. And no one saw it happening.

"She was trying," I said. "She really was."

But something in her got stuck.
Her mind became a maze she couldn't find the way out of. She kept going over everything she'd lost, people, places, pieces of herself, and somewhere in there, she started forgetting who she used to be. It was like being trapped in a room full of broken mirrors, and each reflection showed a version of her she didn't know how to reach anymore. The girl who smiled without faking it. The one who used to believe things could get better. The one who used to feel like enough.

And in that place, she burned.
Not in the way you can see. But inside, she caught fire. Everything she loved about life started turning to ash. Her laughter. Her trust, hope. her light... Gone.

Grief doesn't just take people away.
Sometimes it leaves them behind, but different.

When she finally made it out, she was changed. Not completely, but not the same either. She moved more slowly now. Talked softer. Looked around like the world wasn't real anymore, like she wasn't sure where she belonged in it.

"She didn't vanish," I told them again.
"She burned. And now she's smoke."

Still here. You can see her, but no one can get a hold on her anymore. And if you knew the girl she used to be,
you'd understand why this doesn't feel like her at all.

When the Silence Finally Spoke
(Dissociative Self-Reflection)

She had been silent for a long time. Not the peaceful kind of silence, but the kind that feels heavy inside. It wasn't noisy or angry, just always there, like a shadow she couldn't shake.

She learned early that keeping things inside was safer. If she didn't say what was wrong, nobody could get mad or upset. If she didn't cry or complain, nobody would notice the pain. So she kept it all inside, day after day.
Her friends noticed. "You don't talk much anymore," they said.
She just smiled and said she was fine, talking meant opening up things she wasn't ready to face.

One rainy afternoon, she sat alone at home. The gray light outside made everything feel soft and still. Her phone buzzed with messages, but she ignored them. The emptiness inside her felt louder than any sound.

Then something changed, like a crack in ice. A small word came up from deep inside her: enough.
She said it out loud without thinking. The word echoed in the stillness, breaking something fragile deep within her. She had fought so hard to keep the cracks from showing, and it took everything in her not to fall apart.
But tonight, the weight was too much.
She held it together for as long as she could, but the breaking point was closer than she wanted to admit. She realized she didn't have the strength for pride anymore.

Her hands trembled as she picked up the phone and typed a message to someone she never thought she'd turn to, not after everything.
Not a long story or explanation, just one simple sentence:

I need help.

That was the moment the silence ripped through her, raw and real, and she stopped pretending she was okay.

Come Home
(Fragments of a Life)

He knew he had ruined it. He was the reason she had stopped hoping. He felt it. Not all at once, but in every pause that lasted too long, in the way she skipped over him during conversation, and in the silence that filled every space. Rooms. Rides. Moments. The space between them had once overflowed with laughter, love, kissing, and touching.

Now, the girl who once talked endlessly became her own ghost, drifting toward some version of herself, barely recognized. And the silence got louder. It was no longer protection for her, only something fragile, waiting to break. And it did.

So she spoke.

Not loudly or dramatically. No raised voice. Not even tears. Just words.

"I think," she said, her voice catching, "I'm losing the grip on us."

He did not flinch. Not really. He had already felt it unraveling. Not just her silence, but the way she had begun protecting herself from him a little more each day, until even her presence felt like absence.

"No lies," she added. "No cheating. No pretending."

Afterward, they sat in the stillness that follows a storm.
Even though theirs had never been loud.
It was built from dishonesty and words swallowed in the dark. And when it all went still, it was just her turn to speak.

"I know I was not innocent in the story either," she said. "And after all that happened, I got tired. I pulled back. I became secretive. I stopped giving all of myself. Chose withdrawal instead of begging to be treated right and respected."

"I never meant to hurt you", he said, but not in a way that showed he saw the mess, or what all of his action really cost her.

"You already are," she whispered. "But you can still choose how much."

She waited, but he did not move. No answer. No movement.
Love still ached in her more than before, so she told herself, but only in her head, when we go back, I'm going home. Not to your place, crowded with ghosts and promises never kept. She didn't say it out loud. She kept it inside.

That night, she did not sleep. She kept replaying that horrible thing he did. The one he said out loud a few days ago, maybe by accident, maybe not. It burned into her so deeply that it would not let go. She just lay still. The words echoed like they had nowhere else to land.

After a while, her eyes drifted to the window, where the sky was turning dusky lavender. The color her grandmother always said meant peace was near. But for her, peace was far from close.

The next day, when they arrived, her body was too sick and tired to say anything. She hugged him and looked at him like she already knew how this would end. Yet something in her still wrestled between the part that loved him and the part that remembered all she had endured.

Then his ride came, and he left. She waited for hers, standing in the air between everything unspoken. There was no big goodbye. No last words. Just that kind of leaving that does not look like much, but breaks something inside.

Days blurred after that. Somewhere along the way, she caught something. A cold, maybe. Or a fever. It didn't seem serious. But by the time she got home, it felt worse. She told herself it was all catching up to her.

She stayed in bed, too sick to see him face to face. And when he called, she told him over the phone.

"I'm not coming back to you. I can't let you hurt me anymore. And even though I love you more than you'll ever understand, I have to walk away with whatever dignity I have left. You'll never change for me. You're never going to stand for me. We both know that."

He didn't say much. Just, "I know. Take care of yourself." Then he hung up. As if she were the enemy. The one who wrecked it all.

There was nothing else to say after that. Just the sound of the end. And the silence that stayed with her for a while.

No anger came. She knew him too well for that, so she just held her phone for a long time, then whispered to the room.

"I understand you. I'm not angry. This is just how you make it through. I'll be the villain in your story."

After a few days, her body gave out. It got bad. Fast. Maybe it was a cold...maybe it was everything catching up at once. No one could say for sure if she'd pull through. She drifted in and out for days, whispering a name between shallow breaths.

They said it came fast. But it did not. It started long before. The looking away. The pretending. The way she carried herself like she was not drowning.
Somehow, the people who had loved her the longest found out. They came, sat with her, refuse to leave her side. Said a thousand quiet prayers for her to pull through. They did not need a reason. They were simply there, holding the thread she could no longer reach.

When she opened her eyes, confused, fragile, caught somewhere between leaving and staying, their hands were wrapped around hers like an anchor. Like a promise.

No anger. No questions. Just love. Steady and waiting.
One of them leaned in, eyes full of tears and all the words they could not say out loud, and said: "

Come home, Bella."
Not as a place.
But as a beginning.

If You Want to Stay

A note to those still searching and still holding on

Maybe home isn't a place but a feeling. When you stop pretending and let someone see your real heart, and they don't run. Maybe that won't scare you anymore. Maybe it'll feel like a weight lifting, like finally breathing without holding back.

I don't know when or what it will look like. It might be messy or loud, nothing like the story you've told yourself to survive. But one day, you'll feel it, a steady knowing deep in your bones that says: this doesn't hurt, its feels like something real.

You'll stop shrinking. Stop rehearsing how to leave, and starting to breathe in without holding your breath. That place or person will hold you without asking you to change or hide who you are.

And if you're still lost or numb or worn out, that's okay. Feeling like this doesn't mean you're weak. You've been carrying too much for too long. Just making it through the day is enough, even if it doesn't feel like it.

Remember, not everything or everyone is meant to stay. Some people show up to teach you something, then leave. Some chapters close so you can start a new one, even if it hurts to say goodbye.

Live in this moment. Let go of what's behind you. Tomorrow will come, and you'll be ready and you've been tougher than you thought.

Somewhere out there is a place that won't make you doubt your worth. A place that makes you want to stay.

And I do hope you want to stay.

Power of Truthful Connection

Life with honest people around me feels different. Steady, clear, and real.

There are no guessing games, no reading between the lines, no doubting what's said. You don't have to twist yourself into knots or be dishonest just to uncover the truth.

They speak plainly, without hiding behind masks or half-truths.

It's not always easy; sometimes honesty cuts deep. And their words aren't sugar-coated.

But I respect that It means what they say is real.

It means I'm not living in a fog of uncertainty or second-guessing their intentions. Around honest people, I don't feel the need to protect myself.

I don't have to hide parts of who I am.

I can be open, knowing they'll meet me with the same truth, on the same level. There's a steady kind of trust that builds when honesty is the foundation.

It doesn't mean we always agree or there aren't hard conversations and moments of tension. But even in conflict, things stay real. No games, no pretending.

This kind of life, rooted in truth, respect, and straightforwardness, is what I always wanted. And now it allows me to be myself, fully and without fear.

That kind of clarity and trust makes all the difference...for everyone.

Reflections on The Company We Keep

Someone once told me,

"Your friends represent you. Next time, choose them wisely."

At the time, I brushed it off. Maybe even laughed. It sounded like something bitter people say when they've been burned too many times. But they weren't bitter. They were just telling the truth early.

Life has a way of proving that truth, especially when you're the one left cleaning up someone else's mess. When you find yourself explaining their behavior to others... or worse, explaining it to yourself in the mirror.

You're not always judged for what you do. Sometimes, it's for what the people around you do. Loudly. Publicly. It's all fun and games until their drama becomes your reputation. Until you're the one being side-eyed, questioned, or dropped without a word when someone you let too close lit the match.

That's when it clicks. It's not about how much you like someone. It's about how much they cost you, especially after they betrayed you too.

Reputations are fragile. Guilt by association is real. And loyalty? It's noble...until it turns into self-sabotage.

We like to think we stand on our own. That we're judged solely by our own actions. But the real world doesn't always work that way. People don't see nuance. They see patterns. And if your friends are the chaotic ones, the liars, the users, the betrayers, or the ones stuck in high school games, guess what that makes you look like?

I've learned the hard way. Not everyone deserves a seat at your table. Not that you think you're better than them. You're just tired of paying for their mistakes.

Tired of being collateral damage in someone else's mess. Tired of watching your name take hits for things you never did.

The truth? Most people won't ask for your side of the story. They'll just look at who you spend time with and what those people say about you once you're gone. They'll cast you as the villain and crown themselves the honest ones. All after you stayed quiet.

You keep protecting them, knowing if the full truth ever came out, it wouldn't just destroy them. It would take everything down with them.

And no, it's not fair. But life rarely is.

So now, when I hear
"Your friends represent you." I don't just hear advice.
I hear a warning wrapped in wisdom, the kind you only understand after living it. The wrong company doesn't just speak for you. They speak louder than you ever could.
Yeah, next time I listen and I'll choose more wisely.

In a world where image is everything, the wrong people aren't just dead weight. They're silent character witnesses, testifying against you when you're not even in the room.

With love,
Bella.

The Kindness They Wear

A very wise old man told me a long time ago:

"Bella, do yourself a favor. Stay away from calculated people."

I didn't quite understand, so he explained to me:

Calculated people don't move from the heart. They measure everything: what they give, what they get, what it costs them, and what it gains them. Their kindness has conditions, and their love has an agenda. They don't give from the heart. They give to get a reaction, to protect an image, to secure a return. 'You'll always feel a little off around them, like you're being watched, weighed, maybe even used. You'll question yourself, wondering if you're imagining it. You're not. With them, it's never really about connection. It's about control. So stay close to those who are real, who give without a tally, show up without a motive, and speak with honesty, not strategy.

Those are the people your soul can rest with.

And now?
I understand exactly what he meant.

So here is my version of experience with those kinds of people.

Those people know how to turn heads. How to walk into a room and make people notice. Everything about them is calculated. The way they speak. The way they give. The way they smile…just enough. How people call them generous. Kind. Someone with a good heart. But that's exactly how they want to be seen. It's a role they've mastered. Their kindness isn't born from compassion. It's crafted for effect. But behind the curtain, it's different. When the lights are off and no one's watching, the mask begins to slip. And what's underneath isn't pretty.

They're not driven by love or sincerity. They're driven by the need to be seen as something they're not. The truth? There's a deep, dark loneliness inside them. They never talk about it. An aching emptiness that doesn't go away. No matter how many compliments they collect or how many people smile back at them, they still feel alone.

None of it is about who they truly are. It's all for the mask they've worn for so long, they don't even know what's underneath anymore. Someone cold? Someone empty? Or just tired? They don't let anyone close enough to find out. Or maybe they do, but they're too afraid to face it themselves. Think of that. If they stop pretending, if they finally see who they really are... what happens then? Would anyone still stay?

So they keep the act going.

And their gestures of generosity appear endless, almost effortless.

Bigger smiles. Louder kindness. They speak of love and goodness like they live it, but it's all part of the performance. And people believe it. The illusion is seamless. And it's easier than seeing the truth.

And the darkest part.

What if the mask doesn't just hide them?
What if, after all this time... it's all that's left?

Love,
Bella.

Freedom Sometimes Feels Like Grief

We grow up thinking freedom is the prize. The goal. The big, shining answer. It's supposed to feel like a celebration, the music swelling, the doors flying open, everyone clapping while you step into your new life. But when it finally comes, freedom can hit different. Not like a party. More like an echo. You stand there, keys in hand, looking around and wondering why everything feels so off.

And no one tells you that freedom can feel like loss.
It sounds strange, but having options doesn't always feel like a gift. Sometimes it feels like pressure. Like staring at a blank map with no signs, no rules, no direction. You're finally out of the cage, but now you have to build the next chapter from scratch. And that's terrifying.

You miss the routine. The limits. The way things used to be, not due to them being perfect, but as you knew the rules. Now there are none. You're free to choose, and somehow that freedom is heavier than the chains ever were.
It's like biting into a salad you waited so long for, and it's just dry leaves. No flavor. Just the aftertaste of confusion. You thought it would feel electric. Instead, it feels still in a way that's not peaceful, just empty.

Here's the twist no one tells you. Freedom doesn't always come with joy. Sometimes it walks with grief. And to be free, you have to let go of habits, people, and identities you built just to survive. Even if they weren't right, they were yours. And letting them go hurts more than you expect.

You don't know where to go next. The you, who dreamed of this moment? it's somewhere in the background, still waiting for it all to make sense.
And yet maybe this is what freedom really is. Not fireworks. Not fairy tales. Just this. The space after everything falls away. The ache. The blank page. The terrifying possibility.

But also the wind. So think of an eagle in a storm. It doesn't fight the wind. It rides it, uses the chaos to rise. Maybe freedom is like that too. Not easy. Not clean. But real. Messy. Uncertain. And full of the kind of strength that shows up when you don't know what you're doing but you try anyway.

Be Happy for Real, Not Just Online

Look deep into your soul.

It's so easy to look happy on social media. Just smile in a selfie, pose for a picture, choose the background, slap on a perfectly worded caption, and voilà, instant happiness, right? Except... not really.

Those things don't always mean you're actually happy inside. Sometimes, you get so caught up trying to look like you're living your best life that you forget to live it. Oops.

Real happiness doesn't come from likes, followers, or comments. Shocking, I know. Your loud laugh, your loud acting in front of others, none of that proves your happiness. Who are you trying to fool? Yourself or others? It comes from peace of mind, from good, honest, loving relationships, and from being okay with who you are when no one's watching. Not when you're performing for a screen.

It's laughing with your friends. Feeling proud of how far you've come. Actually doing things by yourself, not by using, asking, or worse, expecting other people to do favors. Imagine that.

And yeah, it's also just enjoying a moment by yourself without needing to announce it.

So, ask yourself this.

When you put the phone down, are you really happy?

If the answer is no, maybe, and I'm just saying maybe, it's time to stop worrying about how happy your life looks online in front of others and start focusing on how it feels in real life.

You don't need to prove nothing to no one. Not when you're miserable inside from the betrayal people caused you.

You don't need to compete either. Let's face it. You can never be them.

So, take care of yourself.

Do things that actually bring you joy, even if no one's watching, clapping, or commenting.

Spend time with people who make you feel loved, not the ones who show up when they're bored, got no one else, or just need to fill the silence.

Make memories for your heart, not just for your feed.

And remember, it's totally fine to share your life.
Just make sure you're actually living it too.

Weight of Shame

One of the heaviest burdens a person can carry is shame, especially the kind that comes from hurting someone who offered nothing but pure, irreplaceable love. Some people, once they realize the damage they've caused, will do everything in their power to make it right, no matter the cost.

To those people: respect.
It takes strength to face your wrongs head-on.

Others, though, choose to hide. They run from the truth, hoping time or distraction will erase the weight they feel. But here's the reality: no matter who they surround themselves with, no matter how much they fake happiness, something will always be missing.

That shame doesn't vanish. It waits. And it hits hardest in the silence of the night, when there's no one left to impress, no noise left to drown it out. It whispers to them in the dark, reminding them of what they lost. And in those moments, lying beside someone who doesn't know the truth, the loneliness inside screams the loudest.

But let's not forget the third kind: the ones who don't feel shame at all. The ones who hurt others and sleep just fine. They're not broken. They're just selfish. Cold. Sometimes…even cruel. And while they may never suffer the way they made others suffer, that says more about who they are than anything else ever could.

Left or Forgotten
(Healing Group Journal)

Someone from my healing group asked me a question they'd seen online:

"What breaks a heart more, being left or being forgotten?"

Honestly, the question was simple, and my answer came without hesitation, so I told them:

Both can break your heart, just in different ways. And sometimes, one can hurt a lot more than the other. It really depends.

When someone chooses to leave you, it's usually after something unforgivable happened. You hurt them deeply, perhaps beyond repair. Something inside them broke. They didn't leave just 'cause they didn't care or love anymore. They left as staying would have meant losing themselves.

So being left breaks your heart like a storm. Sudden. Violent. Unforgettable. They made the choice to walk away, and in that choice, there's pain, but also clarity. You know when it happened, and you know why it happened. You remember the moment. And as much as it hurts, at least the goodbye was heard.

Being forgotten is deeper. Slower. It doesn't shatter the heart. It erodes it. There's no closure, no final word, just silence where once there was meaning. You fade from someone's memory while they still live their lives, laugh their laughs, build their days without you.

It's not just the loss of presence but the loss of significance.

To be left hurts your heart.
To be forgotten makes you question if you ever mattered at all.

And that question haunts longer than any goodbye.

Unspoken Voices

The voices inside are so hushed. I can't get out. I wish I could love myself back to life... but the words won't come. The paper stays empty, mirroring my pain. I can't describe it. My spirit feels shattered, broken into pieces I don't know how to fix.

But even in this stillness, I am here. And maybe, just maybe, this brokenness is where healing begins.
There is a whisper beneath the silence, calling me out for courage, for patience, for time. It tells me I don't have to fix myself all at once, not today. I just need to breathe, to be, to hold myself gently, and trust that even broken things can be made whole again.

So here I am, sitting in this stillness, looking for the moonlight, ready to gather the pieces, one small step, one tender whisper, until the silence turns to words again.

Love,
Bella.

The Gift of His Presence

He doesn't even realize it, but every time we're together, something shifts in me in the best possible way. It's not that he says anything extraordinary or does anything grand. It's just who he is.

His presence has this steady energy that makes me feel safe and understood, like I can take a deeper breath and just be. When I'm around him, I naturally want to be better, not in a performative way, but in a real, grounded sense. I find myself being a little more patient, a little more thoughtful, a little more me.

He brings out parts of me that I sometimes forget about or tuck away: strength I didn't know I had, softness I thought I had to hide, and a sense of calm that's hard to come by these days.

The funny thing is, it's all so effortless. He doesn't try to "fix" me or give advice or impress me. He just shows up as himself, and somehow that's enough to inspire me to show up as my fullest self, too.

And what he gives me is more lasting. It's the way he listens, the way he remembers small things, the way he makes space for me without even realizing it.

It's not about perfection or fairy tales. It's about feeling seen, supported, and truly encouraged just by being with someone who makes you feel like you're already enough and somehow still growing.

When Respect Walks Away
(A Self-Respect Awakening Told Through Emotional Prose)

It's one thing to feel the sting of disrespect in silence, behind closed doors. But when it plays out in front of everyone, when the person you love starts openly flirting with someone else at the same table where you sit, like you're invisible, it cuts in a way words can't explain.

You sit there frozen, ashamed, your face stretched into a fake smile, heart pounding like it's trying to escape your chest. You scan the room, hoping you've misunderstood. But you haven't. Everyone sees it. The laughter. The flirty words. The open glances. None meant for you.

Some people look away, uncomfortable. Others pretend they didn't notice. But a few, just a few, step in, not out of pity. Not to rescue you. They simply know this is not harmless.

So they speak up. Calm. Steady. Telling the other woman and him to back off. No one should be treated like that, especially not in front of the people they love.

He laughs. Says it was nothing. Just playing. But you're not laughing. You see that sharp line between loyalty and betrayal being crossed right there in the open.

You don't fight. You don't cause a scene. You sit still, choking on the tears you refuse to let fall, while your heart breaks into pieces.

Later, you take him outside.

You ask, "Why are you doing this?"

And instead of explaining, comforting, or making it right, he laughs again, looks you in the eye, and says, "Listen, I can have any woman I want. Be grateful it's you."

And in that moment, he makes you feel replaceable. Like your worth depends on his attention, and you should be thankful just to stand beside him.

In that moment, something inside you cracks. Not just the trust or the love. But the part of you that believed he would never make you feel small in public. Your heart doesn't just break. It shatters. He discards your dignity as if it never mattered.

That is when it hits you. He never saw your love as sacred. To him, it was convenient. And now, the man you gave everything to has the nerve to act like you were the lucky one.

But the truth?

He was the one being loved more than he ever deserved. You didn't lose your voice. He lost your respect.

In the Shadow of Loss, She Reached Out for Hope

Only to Be Wounded Again, Worse Than Before

After losing someone she loved, everything changed. The world turned cold. Time moved slowly, but it offered no healing. Grief became a part of her. She learned to carry it, to wear a smile even when her heart remained trapped in the past. The weight of it never lifted, and it seemed she might never feel whole again.

But then, someone returned to her life. He made her believe it was safe to hope, to love, to imagine something good again. And for a while, it felt real, like life was offering another chance.

But behind the warmth and promises, dishonesty crept in. The truth didn't arrive all at once. It came in painful fragments. The same hand that once held hers was now breaking her all over again. This time, it wasn't grief that wounded her. It was something sharper. And somehow, it cut even deeper.

She already knew the ache of losing someone forever, of waking each day with a hollow in her heart. But this betrayal, from someone she had trusted in her most fragile moments, was a different kind of loss.
The pain stayed, but so did her will to keep going.

She wasn't waiting around to be saved anymore. That part of her was done. No one would ever hold that kind of power over her again. What came next wasn't loud or dramatic. Grief had taught her pain. But betrayal, God, betrayal taught her strength.

Broken Roads to Brighter Paths
(Self-reflection)

There were those broken years, on that broken road, with that broken me. The version of myself I barely recognized, carrying too much, saying "I'm fine" far too often, barely holding it together. Everything felt like it was falling apart: dreams unraveling, trust shattered, hope flickering like a candle in the wind. Some days, I didn't know if I'd make it through. But somehow, I did.

Thank goodness I'm not on that road anymore.

Still, every now and then, I find myself looking back. Not to dwell, but to remind myself of what roads not to take, what warning signs to watch for, what patterns to break, and what strength lives in me now as a result of all that pain.

The lessons nearly broke me. The healing was slow. But the growth is real. No one can take that from me.

When I think back about that version of me who kept walking even when it hurt to take the next step, I feel proud. And now, when I look at myself, I see how far I've come since that time.

I Don't Need to Forgive You to Be Whole

People like to say that forgiveness is the key to healing, that it's the only way to move forward, to let go, to be at peace. But I've come to understand something different. I've learned that I don't need to forgive you in order to be okay. My peace, my growth, even my healing, they don't depend on whether or not I let go of what you did. They depend on me and only me.

> Forgiveness is often painted as a moral obligation, as if I don't offer it, I'm the one carrying bitterness or stuck in the past. But the truth is, I have moved forward. I've built myself back up, faced the pain, sat with it, understood it, and made something out of it. You don't get to be part of that process just *'cause* you were part of the damage.

What happened hurt. Maybe you didn't mean to, maybe you did. It doesn't matter anymore. The point is, I've felt every inch of that hurt. I've cried over it, but eventually, I found ways to live around it. And now I'm living beyond it. That's healing. That's wholeness. And it didn't require me to hand you some ribbon-wrapped forgiveness to make it legitimate.

Forgiveness is not a shortcut to closure. It's not a box I need to check off to prove I've grown. I don't owe anyone that, not even myself, if it's not what I truly feel.

Maybe one day I will forgive you. Maybe I won't. But either way, that decision is mine. Not forgiving you doesn't mean I'm stuck, bitter, or small. It means I'm honest about my boundaries. It means I'm allowed to protect myself in the ways that feel right to me.

I don't need to carry your guilt, your story, or your need for redemption. That's not mine to hold. My wholeness, my worth, my peace, those are mine. And they were never tied to whether I forgive you or not.

So no, I don't need to forgive you. And I'm still whole without that.

Let's Talk: What's the Fastest Way to Get Over Someone?
(Healing Group Journal)

A few members in my healing group are struggling to move on from their past relationships.

So let's dive in.
How do you get over someone fast?

And I don't mean blocking their number or deleting pictures. That's surface-level digital damage control. Pretending you're fine while still checking their stories. I'm talking about real healing. The kind that doesn't just cover the wound. It closes it yet a big part of you is still aching. Still waiting for a text that isn't coming. Still replaying moments, rewriting the past, thinking maybe if you'd just said the right thing.

Here's the truth:
There is no fast way. No magic button. No shortcut.

But there is a real way if you're willing to go deep. And that way hurts like hell before it heals.

First, stop romanticizing what was.
It wasn't perfect. If it were, you wouldn't be here.
Don't just remember the butterflies. Remember the confusion. The waiting. The unmet needs. The gut feeling you ignored. Grieve the future you thought you'd have. Then, slowly, stop editing the story to make them the hero. Stop making excuses for what broke you.

Sit in the silence. Don't rush to fill it. Don't numb it with someone new. Let it echo. Let it hurt. Let it teach you what you truly need, what you overlooked, what you gave up just to keep them.

Start remembering the moments you felt small.
When you stayed quiet to keep the peace.

When you poured love into someone who only held out a paper cup.

Then forgive yourself. Not for loving them, but for staying too long. For hoping they'd change. For shrinking yourself. For offering your heart to someone who never knew how to hold it.

And after that, you turn inward.
You show up for yourself the way they never did.
Take yourself out. Write what you never said. Move your body. Clean your space. Call your friends back. Let them love you, especially the messy, healing parts.
Remind yourself daily that letting go isn't failure. It's freedom.

And one day, without realizing it, you'll wake up and notice you haven't thought about them in weeks. You don't check their page. You don't rehearse conversations.
You just breathe.

So no, there's no shortcut. But if you're brave enough to feel it instead of avoid it, you'll move through it faster than you think. Time doesn't do the heavy lifting. You do.

So what's the fastest way to get over someone?
It's not deleting them from your phone.
It's grieving the version of you that kept settling for almost and empty promises.

Already Gone Before He Left
(A Voice For The Betrayed)

It's easy for a man to walk away when he stopped loving you long before he walked out. When he had already been living a double life, telling you what you wanted to hear while giving his real intentions to someone else, his body was beside you, but his loyalty had already left the room.

By the time he finally leaves, it's not a shock. It's the slow truth rising to the surface, the moment your heart catches up to what it always knew but never wanted to believe. That he had already let go. That he had already chosen another life, another woman, another version of himself, where you no longer existed.

What hurts most isn't the moment he walked away. It's how he stayed. How he kissed and touched other women, then came home and kissed you like nothing had changed. Touched you like you were the only one. Held you while hiding everything. He looked you in the eyes while knowing he belonged somewhere else. And every time he crossed that line behind your back, he took another piece of the truth with him.

That kind of pain, the one that sits in your chest like a weight, isn't just about losing him. It's about realizing you were holding on to something he had already thrown away. It wasn't just the end of a relationship. It was the slow unraveling of your spirit, moment by moment, every time he smiled and lied in the same breath, from loving someone who had already stopped being yours in every way that mattered.

It may feel like you lost everything when he left. But the truth is, you didn't lose a real partner. You lost someone who had been gone long before he ever said goodbye. And one day, you'll look back and see that you were always the one who stayed honest, present and true.

Then you'll understand you weren't left behind. You were set free.

You're Not the Girl Who Came Out Clean

They say; you survived. That should be enough. But some days, it doesn't feel like survival. It feels like wreckage. Like you made it out of the fire, but the fire didn't leave you.

People want a clean ending. You left. You healed. You're better now. Sometimes you let them believe that. Saying I left, but I still carry him, that's harder. Not by choice. Trauma clings. It marks everything.

Soft voices make you flinch. Kindness makes you question. Silence makes you brace. You don't always recognize the girl in the mirror. She made it, but she carries what doesn't show.

You didn't walk away with grace. You broke. You stayed. You believed him and you blamed yourself.

You carry the shame like it's part of you, not just for what happened, but for how much it still hurts. Even now. Even free. You hear him in the pauses. The apologies for existing slip out for no reason, how you shrink without meaning to.

This is the part no one talks about:
The after. The raw, slow, ugly after. When you're free but not healed, you have to relearn your own voice.
When you whisper we're safe now, even though your body still flinches and healing feels like breaking again, just softer this time.

No, you're not the girl who came out clean.
But you came out. And that's a strength.

Forgotten What Safe Felt Like

You forgot what safe felt like. It slipped through your fingers and disappeared deep inside, leaving only a shadow when you reach for it. Trauma doesn't just shake you; it rewires everything: the beat of your heart, the way your mind trusts, even how your body breathes. Peace becomes a stranger you once knew but no longer recognize.

Before trauma, safety might have been simple: a warm room, a steady voice, a hand that stayed. Afterwards, your senses sharpen in all the wrong ways. You listen for threats in silence. You scan the room without thinking. Home stops feeling like home. Everything becomes a test you're scared to get wrong. Your brain doesn't settle. It stays ready. It learned the hard way that nothing was ever really safe. Trust feels like something that gets you hurt.

You want peace, but it never feels close enough. And when it does, your body locks up and pushes it away. You try to settle, but something inside pulls tight. One time you let yourself relax and it cost you everything. Now even calm moments make you flinch.

This rewiring isn't just mental; it's in your bones. You flinch when someone gets too close. Your chest tightens at sudden sounds. Your mind jumps to worst-case scenarios before you even realize. It's exhausting to live like this. You want to believe safe is real, but you don't even remember how it feels to breathe easily, to sleep without dread.

Yet inside the broken wiring, a faint pulse remains, a stubborn hope. Maybe one day that pulse will grow louder. Maybe, safe will stop being a ghost and become something real again. Forgetting safe doesn't mean you've lost it forever. It means your wounds run deep, and healing is teaching your heart to trust again, slowly, piece by piece, in a world that hasn't been kind.

So even if safe feels like a stranger now, know this: it's still out there, waiting. One day you might find it, not perfect, not without scars, but for real.

I Lost Myself Trying to Hold On
(Emotional Vulnerability)

I lost friends. People I once thought were my ride or die. The kind of friends you believe will be with you through anything, the ones who'll have your back no matter what... until everything changed.
And in the middle of all that, I lost myself.

I was betrayed, lied to, and played with so much that I started questioning my own reality, my own sanity. I couldn't even trust my own thoughts anymore. Everything I believed in was being torn apart right in front of me. It was like living in a constant fog where nothing made sense and every truth felt like a lie in disguise.

Don't get me wrong. I'm not trying to paint myself as a victim or act like I'm some kind of saint. I'm not. I'm far from perfect. I've got my own mess, my own flaws, and I definitely played my part in everything that happened. I made mistakes and choices that I'm not proud of. I said things, did things, and allowed things that hurt me in the end.

Put myself in situations I knew weren't good for me. Stayed in places where I wasn't respected. Gave chances to people when they weren't deserved. And slowly, piece by piece, I broke down. Until there was almost nothing left. I became mentally exhausted and physically sick. My body and mind just couldn't take it anymore.

I hit a point where I was just one inch away from giving up on everything, on life, on hope, on myself.

Those people, those so-called friends, those connections I thought were solid, they broke me. They truly did. But here's the part that hurts the most: I can't even fully blame them. I can't point fingers and say it was all their fault. And if I'm being honest, if I really look at the truth, the person I have to blame is myself.

I let them break me.
I gave them the power. Ignored every red flag. Silenced my own voice, just to keep the peace. Stayed when I knew damn well I should've left.
And in doing that, I lost myself.

You Bury Your Past

When you bury your past, do it with both hands.
Don't flinch. Don't look back. Call it by a name only you will recognize, then let that name vanish.

Pile the dirt high. Let it hurt. Let the weight press down until you feel clean. Leave no markers, no flowers. Walk away like it never belonged to you.

Carry the lesson in your spine, where it makes you stand taller. Not in your chest, where it can bruise. And once it's buried, don't linger near the ground. Don't visit out of habit or answer questions about where it went.

There are people who return to the site just to see if it stirs.
They crave the echo, not the silence. Misery makes them feel at home. Your healing threatens the grip they once had.

Guard what grew from it. Protect the quiet things that came after.
Your peace is not a shrine. It owes no one an explanation. And no one gets the map back to your pain.

Sleep Wasn't Rest, It Was Escape
(Self-Reflection)

Sleep wasn't rest. It was a place I ran to when everything else hurt too much to face. I didn't close my eyes, hoping for peace or healing. I closed them to shut out the noise in my head. The constant replay of things I wish I could forget. The weight of loneliness lodged in my chest. The ache of feeling invisible and broken.

But even in sleep, I wasn't free. My body stayed tense and alert, like it was waiting for something bad to happen. My heart pounded. My breath stayed shallow. My mind refused to quiet. It chased me through the dark, dragging memories and fears behind it. I woke up more exhausted than before. pain doesn't stop when your eyes are closed.

People told me to rest, and recharge. But I wasn't resting. I was hiding. Hiding from the anger. Hiding from the fear I couldn't say out loud. Hiding from the parts of me that felt too broken to fix. It was the only time I could fall apart without anyone watching.

But falling apart isn't the same as healing. Every morning, I opened my eyes to the same weight pressing down on me. I felt empty and heavy all at once, like I was carrying scars no one could see. I kept hoping sleep would be my escape. But it was only a pause between moments of pain.

I don't know how long I kept running. Using sleep like a shield. But I do know this: running doesn't heal you. Sometimes, even rest is just another way to avoid the truth waiting for you when you wake up.

Hidden Faces of Malice

Malicious people are often hidden in plain sight. They smile in your face, speak sweet words, and act like they're on your side, but deep down, they harbor intentions to pull you down. They thrive on gossip, manipulation, and stirring up trouble, feeding off the mess they create. Their goal is to weaken your confidence, shake your sense of peace, and make you question yourself.

They can be strangers, friends, family, or even those you once trusted with your heart. Their words are sharp in disguise, their actions subtle but calculated, all designed to create doubt, isolation, and division.

They are toxic, and project their misery outward, hoping to find control by dimming someone else's light. Their mess is a reflection of their own emptiness. But you don't have to let that be your reality.

You have the power to step out of the chaos, to stay strong, to keep your boundaries firm, and to protect your energy with intention. You are under no obligation to engage with their negativity, to stoop to their level, or to prove yourself to people who are committed to misunderstanding you.

Their power over you only exists if you allow it.

Always remember this: the people who truly matter, the ones with good hearts and steady hands, will support you, uplift you, and see your worth clearly, even when others try to distort it with lies and cruelty.

Focus on building a life rooted in kindness, truth, and respect. Nurture relationships that feel safe and real. And let the malicious fade into the background where they belong, irrelevant to your growth, your peace, and your future.

But no matter how loudly they scheme in the shadows, your truth will always speak louder, and you will always outshine their darkness.

When the Strong One Speaks
(Healing Group Journal)

One day, during a weekly conversation with my healing group, a few of the members asked me about my fears.

And even though I'm supposed to be one of the strong ones, the one who holds space for them, I opened up.

I told them how, sometimes, I still feel invisible and unheard. Not good enough to be helping them. Not good enough, maybe, to be helping anyone.

They didn't say much.
The silence was loud.

The next day, I received this message.
This is what they wrote:

That feeling of being invisible, of thinking your presence doesn't matter, is a heavy kind of pain. Pain often hides from us. Even if someone didn't see your worth doesn't mean it isn't there. You matter. Your impact has always mattered. Maybe not to the people who failed to show it, but that doesn't make it any less real. Especially when it feels like no one sees you, your existence has already left giant ripples behind: A kind word you said. *Your ability to make people feel seen, heard, laugh, and make them believe they're worth it. A moment, someone (including all of us) feels less alone any time you show up.* These things live on, whether or not they're spoken out loud.

Message written by Annam Healing Group members.

So here I am, with tears.
And I am so deeply honored and proud of each and every one of them. From the very first day they joined my group, they've carried wisdom, heart, and healing in ways that continue to leave me in awe.

Love,
Annam

Christmas Greetings from My Healing Group
(Healing Group Journal)

Dear Annam,

We just wanted to take a moment to thank you. Truly. Being part of this group has changed us in ways we didn't even know we needed.

From the very beginning, you created something special. A space where we felt safe enough to be honest, messy, open, and real. You never judged or rushed us. You let us be exactly who we are. And somehow, that made us feel like we could finally breathe.

You've built more than just a healing group. You've built a kind of sanctuary. A place where everybody could fall apart and still feel whole. A place where our stories were heard, not just with ears, but with a kind of understanding that's hard to find in this world.

You've shown us that healing doesn't have to happen alone. That we're not broken. Just growing. Your strength, your patience, your willingness to be vulnerable with us... it's moved us more than you know.

You didn't just guide us. You walked beside us. And in doing so, you helped us remember who we are beneath the pain.

We've made it through a lot this year. The love, the ugly cries, the belly laughs, and everything in between. We're still crying, still healing, but somehow laughing more, starting to be okay... and now, some of us are even helping others find their way too.

You and your helpers stayed alongside with us. Even when we were ready to give up, and it felt like everyone else already had, you didn't. You stayed. You reminded us what it means to be held, even in the mess.

We carry everything you've given us. Your words, your kindness, your light. As we keep moving forward. No matter where life takes us, this space you created will always be a part of us.

Merry Christmas and Happy New Year.
Your (slightly dramatic but really touched) Healing Group.

The Pieces You Needed to Let Go

They'll never understand how many versions of you had to vanish just so this one could survive.

All the times you had to shrink to fit, to pretend you were fine when you were breaking inside.
The moments you stayed silent while your soul was screaming.

They won't see the nights you cried alone or the choices that felt like survival, even when they chipped away at your heart.

They don't know about the dreams you buried, the friendships you need to let go of, or the parts of yourself you had to unlearn just to feel safe in your own skin.

You've reshaped yourself time and time again, not for attention or applause, but staying the same would have meant slowly disappearing.

And now here you are, still healing, still growing, still breathing. Not perfect, but finally becoming someone who feels like you.

And they'll never really know what it cost to become you.

You Are What You Go Back For

You learn a lot by watching what others crawl back to. Not for love or closure. Just something they're ashamed to admit in front of the world.

Said it was over. Made sure everyone knew. The dramatic kind of ending people clapped for. Strong. Final. Public. Which made the secret return visits easier to hide. Sometimes midday or afternoon, so the daytime disappearances didn't raise suspicion.

The blinds stayed shut. Not many words exchanged. Nothing tender. Just old muscle memory and a silence that didn't ask questions.

Nothing lingered after. Just the sound of getting dressed, and for one of them, a very well-hidden, deep emptiness.

The whole story had been passed around. The worst parts retold over wine and sympathy.

And still, the visits keep happening. Not for comfort or reconnection. For something smaller. Temporary happiness, the excitement of secrecy. Something low enough to crawl back to without saying a word.

True, it's a secret, but not the thrilling kind. It's the one dragged behind like a stain.

Too shameful to admit, if only anyone knew what it's really for, there'd be no sympathy left. Just the kind of judgment reserved for people who put themselves beneath what they swore they'd never accept again, and still go back.

The Silence After Struggle

Ever notice how silent it gets when you're not okay?

Not the peaceful kind. The other one. The kind that hums with discomfort. The one where people who once laughed the loudest with you suddenly go quiet, unsure of what to say. You're in a room full of people, but somehow it still feels empty.

It's like pain makes everyone uneasy, like your honesty is a mirror they'd rather not look into. You try to speak, say you're tired, overwhelmed, barely holding it together, and instead of comfort, you get distance. The mood shifts. Eyes drop. Phones come out. Conversations take a sharp turn toward lighter things. They offer advice, distractions, or nothing at all, but rarely real presence.

And maybe it's not cruelty. Maybe it's fear. Maybe your pain brushes up against theirs, and they're not ready to feel it. Or maybe they just don't know how to sit with what can't be fixed.
But it still hurts to feel invisible when all you really need is to be seen.

Still, the silence has something to teach you. It shows you who's only there when you're easy to be around. It teaches you how to hold yourself together when no one else knows how. And most of all, it makes you treasure the rare ones, the people who stay, who sit with your mess without flinching, who don't need you to be okay to still choose you.

No One to Blame

You ask, "Who can I blame?" But deep down, you already know the answer: no one, really. You took the risk with your eyes wide open, hoping for something that might be worth the fall. That hope, that belief, wasn't weakness. It was courage.

You stayed, even when it hurt. The reason is simple. It mattered to you. And there's nothing shameful about that.

The hard truth is, sometimes we reach for something already slipping away. Not from foolishness. Hope pulls hard. You cared. You gave what you had. That was real.

What hurts the most isn't the ending. It's standing here now, feeling how much of yourself is still tangled in what never became anything solid.

If blame belongs anywhere, maybe it's in the silence when you needed words. In the indifference, you met when you gave your all. But don't put it all on yourself. Grief wants someone to blame. Healing doesn't. Healing needs honesty, and you've already taken that first step.

Smiles in Front, Knives Behind
(How Charming!)

Some people smile at you like you're best friends, then the moment you turn your back, they're talking like you're their worst enemy.
Adorable, right?

Two-faced people are everywhere. They act sweet, supportive, even loyal, but only when it benefits them. Very generous.
They wear their masks so well, you almost forget who they really are.
Such talented performers.

But actions always speak louder than fake smiles, unless you're into theater. In that case, enjoy the show.

They'll laugh with you today, then laugh at you tomorrow. Multitaskers! They'll pretend to care when others are watching. How noble of them. But deep down, they're rooting for your downfall. Apparently, your success is just too hard for them to handle.

And no, it's not always jealousy. Sometimes, it's just who they are: malicious, insecure, bitter, and hollow.
So relatable.

Eventually, you learn to spot them. The ones who vanish when you need them.
Classic.

The ones who talk more about you than to you. Great communication skills. The ones who only clap when it's convenient.
True supporters, obviously.

And when you do? Don't fight them. Don't expose them. Just distance yourself. Let them drown in their own fakeness while you keep growing, quietly, steadily, unapologetically.

But hey, let's wish them the best... while they secretly hope for our worst.

The Kind of Love You Finally Chose

In the end, you didn't go with the one who saw your strength as a threat, or your independence as something to tame. You walked away from the kind of love that made you shrink so he could feel bigger.

Instead, you found a man whose ego doesn't demand your peace as a sacrifice, with whom you can fully be a woman.
Not fooled into calling control care, or silence respect.

Who listens not just to reply, but to genuinely understand the mind behind your words. A partner who doesn't need to win every argument, for he values building something with you more than proving something to himself or worse, to everyone else.

This is the kind of love that gives you space to exhale.
You're no longer expected to translate your feelings just to be taken seriously. The messy, complicated, human parts of you are met with grace, not scrutiny. Your softness isn't turned against you, and strength isn't something he resents.

Most of all, love stopped feeling like survival.
You were finally allowed to be fully, unapologetically you.

But after everything you've endured and everything you've outgrown, that kind of love is nothing short of revolutionary.

The Silence That Said Everything

He never gave you the chance to know. Honesty was never on his agenda. If you hadn't uncovered the truth yourself, he would have kept living like nothing was wrong, like you didn't deserve to hear it.

And that's what shatters you the most. Not just what he did, but the fact that he deliberately kept you in the dark. As if you weren't even worth the truth. In that instant, your whole world crumbles, like the ground just disappeared beneath your feet.

You're left clutching the broken pieces of your heart while the silence of his lies screams louder than any confession ever could. The worst wound isn't the betrayal itself. It's the cold reality that he didn't respect you enough to be honest. That kind of deception cuts deeper than anything. It's not only about what he did. It's about what he chose to withhold. The one simple thing he failed at: telling you the truth.

And in that silence, you grasp an even harsher truth. The real pain isn't the lies, but the silence that screams he never truly cared enough to be real with you.

But listen closely. Right now, you're sitting in the aftermath of all of it. Everything feels heavier than it should. You're carrying what he left behind with no way to make sense of it. There is no fix no fast way out. Just time and the slow process of learning how to live with what you know now. You need to understand, you won't stay in this place forever. Even it feels endless, it's not. You will move through it. Not cleanly not without a scar but far enough to see he never had the power to define your Worth. You'll be OK even from this broken place.

Silent Collapse

Lately, everything hurts in ways you can't explain, no matter how many times you've tried. God knows you've tried. But every time you open up, they look at you like you're broken. Like you're a burden. Like your pain is too much, too messy, too inconvenient.

So you stop. You shut down. You carry it all in silence, like you're being punished just for feeling. And still, people say, "You seem fine." Yeah. what's the point of falling apart when no one's going to catch you?

So you cry in the shower. You scream into pillows.
You lie awake at 4 a.m., staring at the ceiling, wondering how you're still here, how you keep waking up when all you want is for everything to stop.

But what breaks you most isn't the pain itself. It's that no one sees it. Worse, no one wants to.

You could be bleeding on the inside, and they'd still ask you to smile. Expect you to show up and call you "strong" for not making a scene they'd have to deal with.

But inside?

You already have.

When Someone Messes With Your Head: Gaslighting and the Hot and Cold Game

Have you ever felt like you're losing your mind, even though you know perfectly well you're not? One day, someone acts like you're the center of their universe. Then, you're suddenly invisible, like a ghost at a party. That's not just confusing. It's emotional manipulation doing its sneaky thing.

Gaslighting is when someone tries to rewrite your reality. They might say things like, "That never happened," "You're overreacting," or "You always misunderstand." Before long, you start doubting your own memory and feelings. You might even wonder if you're the problem. Spoiler alert: you're not.

Then there's the classic "hot and cold" treatment. One minute they're warm and sweet. Next, they're distant and icy. You're left scratching your head, trying to figure out what you did wrong. Newsflash: probably nothing.

These tricks leave you anxious, insecure, and emotionally exhausted. It's like they're dangling just enough kindness to keep you hooked, but never enough to make you feel safe or truly valued.

Here's the real deal
Consistency isn't too much to want. Being seen and heard shouldn't feel like a luxury. Love should be steady. Real.
The kind that doesn't hurt. And respect is the bare minimum.

If someone keeps playing mind games or makes you feel like you're tiptoeing through a minefield, it's not your fault and it's totally okay to walk away. Your peace matters more than their drama.

You're So Broken and You Don't Even Know What to Do Anymore

Some days, it feels like you're completely shattered inside, like every part of you is cracked and splintered, and good luck trying to figure out where to start putting yourself back together. You wake up feeling heavy, like there's a stubborn elephant sitting on your chest that refuses to move. You try to push through, but honestly, you just don't know what to do anymore. The things that once made sense? Yeah, they've gone on vacation.

You're stuck in this weird, foggy place where everything feels confusing and overwhelming, and you're scared to take the next step not knowing if it'll help or just make the mess worse. It's like wandering through a maze in the dark, except someone forgot to bring a flashlight. And maybe the hardest part? *Admitting you're broken, even though somewhere deep down, you thought by now you'd have it all figured out.* Spoiler alert: You don't. And that's perfectly okay.

You don't have all the answers. No master plan. Just this messy, imperfect moment, and maybe, just maybe, that's enough. You're discovering it's okay to be lost and uncertain. It doesn't mean you're weak or failing; it means you're human.

Sometimes the best move is to just breathe, let yourself feel the pain (yes, even the ugly kind), and trust that somehow, slowly, you'll find your way back. One tiny step at a time.

And here's a secret: in all this brokenness, there's a weird kind of strength, the kind that keeps you showing up on the hardest days, even when you can't see the road ahead. So even if it feels like you're stuck in a never-ending episode of "What Now?" remember, this moment won't last forever. You will heal. You will find your light again. Just give yourself permission to be exactly where you are.

Silent Shards

She gazes into the mirror, something she usually avoids, and wonders about the fractured reflection staring back at her. No one has seen it. No one has noticed just how deeply she's splintered herself from the inside out, piece by piece.

What remains is a fragile will to survive, a desperate focus on simply staying alive. The truth is, she still doesn't know how to heal, how to mend the cracks, or how to feel whole again.

Every day is a battle. And though she wears her mask well, inside she's still lost, still searching for a way back to herself.

But maybe the fact that she keeps searching means she hasn't given up. Maybe buried beneath the damage is a flicker of something more, something that still believes healing is possible.

Where Do You Turn?
(Self-Trust)

They asked her:

"Where do you turn when you're unsure?"

She said,

I close my eyes. I look inward and listen to the hum of my nervous system. Three guides live within me: intuition, values, and wisdom.
They never lie. They know me best. So, I follow them.
When I'm lost, I don't look outside myself.

Each of those three within me speaks a truth no map can show. *None of them ever lead me wrong.*

So I listen. I feel. I trust.
They always show the way forward.

Sleep Not Enough

Sometimes, sleep feels like putting a Band-Aid on a broken leg; it looks like you're trying, but absolutely nothing is getting fixed. You lie down, close your eyes, and pretend it's all going to melt away. But no. Your brain decides it's the perfect time to replay every awkward conversation you've ever had since 2007.

Sleep isn't rest; it's just nightly amnesia with commercials. You drift off, hoping for peace, but instead, your mind runs a full-length horror documentary titled Cringe: The Greatest Hits. And somehow, it's always on a loop.

What you really need? Not eight hours. Not melatonin. You need a full system reboot. A selective memory wipe. Something between a nap and a lobotomy, just enough to forget your ex, your childhood haircut, and whatever you said to your boss when you were sleep-deprived and overconfident.

So yeah, rest is nice... but forgetting? Forgetting is bliss.

Spaces Between Words

It was late. The kind of late where the world softens, and even the streetlights seem unsure of themselves. We sat on that cold bench outside my house. Neither of us looked at the other. We just sat there, close but not touching, as if any movement might shatter the fragile stillness we'd built around ourselves.

I wanted to say something. Anything.

That I didn't know how we got here... That I hated how silence had become our only language. That the weight of unsaid things was starting to bruise.

But the words were stuck somewhere between my heart and my throat. Too heavy to carry, too fragile to drop.

You didn't speak either.

Instead, you reached out and took my hand. Just that. No drama. No tears. Just fingers slipping into mine, tentative at first, then sure. And in that one simple gesture, everything unraveled. The distance. The unresolved arguments. The slow accumulation of days spent not fully connecting.

It all came rushing in and then out without a single sound.

Your thumb traced circles on my skin, slow and steady. I felt the apology there. The ache. I felt you, not the version you showed the world, but the real you. The one who still hoped.

We sat like that for a long time. Not speaking. Not needing to.

And sometimes, a hand in yours says more than any sentence ever could. And in that stillness, I think we both understood:
Some connection survives in the spaces between.

With love,
Bella.

When Your Own Voice Betrays Your Heart

The saddest sound I know is the fragile crack in someone's voice just before tears fall, that vulnerable break that reveals the pain they're desperately trying to hide. It's a silent scream, impossible to put into words. You want to comfort them, to ease the ache, but all you can do is listen.

What makes it even more heartbreaking is when that crack comes from your own voice. When you're fighting to stay composed, to hold yourself together, and suddenly your voice falters and breaks. In that moment, the walls you built around your heart begin to crumble.

Hearing yourself break is like looking into a mirror that reflects not only your face but the chaos inside, the heartbreak, the loss, the weight that feels impossible to carry. It's proof that even the strongest can fracture.

And sometimes, the hardest truth to embrace is that breaking is part of healing. And within that trembling voice, in that delicate crack, lies the very beginning of recovery.

Missing Yourself

Have you ever found yourself missing who you once were?
Not just a moment or a memory, but the real you. The version that felt lighter, smiled more easily, and laughed without holding back. The one who moved through life with a fierce spark, a kind of glow that wasn't about pictures or appearances, but something you felt deep inside. In your chest, your eyes, and even in how people noticed your energy when you entered a room.

You catch yourself wondering when that part of you started to drift away. Did it happen slowly, almost without you noticing? Or did life hit you hard all at once and take it away in a flash? You can't quite tell. But you know something has shifted. You sense it in your body, in the way your inner voice sounds, in the tired way you get through the day.

And when you look in the mirror, you think, "I miss that person." Not that you don't care about who you are now, but you remember what it was like to feel whole. Alive with hope, with belief that things could be different. And now, it feels like you're just surviving, putting one foot in front of the other.

Here's the thing: that person is still there. Not lost. Not gone forever. Maybe just quieter for now. Waiting patiently. You don't have to force your way back or pretend everything's fine. You just have to show up for yourself in small ways. Take the little steps. Rest when you need it. Say no to what wears you down. Say yes to moments of joy, even if they feel strange or unfamiliar.

You don't need to rewind time to find yourself again. You only need to clear a little room for your own comeback. And you will. You're already on your way.

So maybe next time, when you catch your reflection, you'll see it. That flicker of who you were. Not as a memory. But as someone returning home.

Connection vs. Attachment

There's a difference between connection and attachment, and most people never truly grasp it. Connection is rare. It's the kind of bond that fuels you, that gives you strength even when everything else feels like it's falling apart. It's mutual, balanced, and somehow freeing. When you're connected, you feel alive, supported, and even a little invincible.

Attachment, by contrast, is a trap disguised as something meaningful. It clings like a weight, draining your energy until you're left hollow and exhausted. Attachment isn't about freedom or strength; it's about need and fear. It's holding on too tightly to something or someone who may never give back what you're pouring in. The worst part? You convince yourself it's love, necessity, or fate when really it's just a slow bleed.

Many confuse the two out of fear of loneliness or crave the feeling of being needed. But attachment drains you while connection empowers you. One leaves you depleted; the other makes you stronger. Recognizing the difference is brutal, but it's the only way to protect yourself from getting lost in the wrong ties. This isn't just wisdom. It's survival.

I Protect My Peace by Refusing to Tolerate Hypocrisy (Personal Reflection)

I've decided to step back, not out of judgment but out of self-respect. I noticed a pattern that unsettles me: constant gossip filled with judgment and negativity behind people's backs, followed by everyone sitting at the same table, smiling and pretending everything is fine, as if nothing had happened. That kind of dynamic feels exhausting and insincere.

Trust shouldn't be so easily broken, only to be covered up with surface-level kindness and pretense. This isn't about holding grudges or thinking I'm better than anyone. It's about guarding my peace and choosing authenticity over façades.

I want to be around people who mean what they say and say what they mean. I value spaces where communication is straightforward and respect is steady, both in private and in public.

This is how I protect my peace. I choose sincerity, transparency and genuine connection over the illusion of harmony without honesty.

From Worn Down to Worthy
(Personal Reflection)

My last relationship made me feel old. Not just in my heart, but in the way I looked. I saw it in the deep lines that hadn't been there before, the tired look in my eyes, the way my shoulders sagged without me even realizing. I stopped talking. I stopped being myself.

I carried the weight of every argument, every broken promise. There were a lot of them. They left marks no one else could see, but I felt them every single day. I spent too many nights worrying instead of resting, crying instead of sleeping, always bracing for the next wave of tension. It wore me out, body and soul.

When I looked in the mirror, I didn't even recognize the person staring back. It wasn't time that aged me, it was everything I'd been through. My eyes didn't shine the way they used to. A part of me that once burned with energy, dreams, and hope had gone dim. I forgot what it felt like to wake up excited for the day, to look forward to what was ahead.

What hurt the most was that I never expected this. I wanted love that made me stronger, not something that drained me. But instead, I felt empty, like a faded version of the woman I used to be.

Somewhere deep down, I always knew this wasn't how it was meant to be. Life should be more than just making it through the day. I wanted someone who would stand beside me, someone who'd see the fire in me and help it burn brighter. I wanted to look in the mirror and see strength again, to feel alive, to chase after the things that set my soul on fire.

But along the way, that fire started fading. So when that relationship made me feel older than I was, I realized something was wrong.

I had to ask myself: am I going to keep losing pieces of who I am, or is it time to choose myself?

Real love should never leave me feeling small. It shouldn't silence me, wear me out, or embarrass me in front of others. That's not care, that's control. And I am not here to be anyone's lesson or burden. I want someone grounded, respectful, and grown enough to keep what we build between us.

And when something is wrong between us, we fix it together. Just two of us. Not other women, a group chat, followers, and online friends. Just us. Figuring out together. Not with others involved.

The Return of Joy and What Love Really Is

Sometimes, a person steps into your life and changes everything. They fill the cracks you didn't know existed and bring back a joy you forgot was possible. They make you laugh again. They make you feel truly seen. And without even trying, they help you believe in love again.

It doesn't happen all at once. Words don't always line up, but somehow, you begin to understand each other in the small things: a smile, a look, a shared silence. Love isn't about what's said. It's about feeling safe, understood, and like you finally belong.

And then, in those unspoken moments, it all begins to make sense. With the right person, the overthinking fades. You stop chasing. You just are. And that's more than enough. They don't bring chaos. They bring peace. They don't fix you. You were never broken. They remind you of your strength and your dreams. The future with them feels like a promise, not a gamble.

You laugh more. Breathe easier. Carry less. Not as a result of life being perfect, it just feels real. Even in silence, you're heard. Even in disagreement, you're safe. Being with them makes everything lighter.

Love isn't a test or a challenge. It's coming home. They don't change you. Just remind you who you are and walk beside you as you become who you're meant to be.

Silence Spoke Louder Than Words

The house felt different the next morning. Still. Heavy. Not just a silence that fills a room, but one that presses down on your chest. I kept waiting to hear his footsteps, that familiar laugh from the other room, the small habits you only recognize as sacred once they're gone.

Losing someone you love doesn't happen all at once. There's the sharp, final moment, but the real loss unfolds slowly, in waves. It's in the coffee mug left on the counter, the phone number you can't bring yourself to delete, the impulse to call followed by the brutal reminder that no one will answer.

Grief doesn't ask permission. It slips into conversations, creeps into dreams, and appears unexpectedly on roads you've traveled a thousand times. And yet, somehow, we learn to carry it, not by getting over the loss, but by growing strong enough to bear its weight.

The world keeps spinning. Indifferent. Relentless. And we keep going with it, carrying what we can't forget

With love,
Bella.

Only When It's Convenient

Ever notice how some people develop selective memory? They forget you exist right up until they need something.

Suddenly, you're their favorite person. The texts roll in. The calls come through. You're the go-to. Not that they miss you. They just know you're useful. But when the roles reverse? Crickets. Radio silence. Everyone's mysteriously busy.

It's a gut-punch kind of truth: being there for people who vanish the second you need something back. It's not that you expect payback. You just want to feel like you matter beyond your ability to help, fix, or listen.

Here's the thing: being remembered only when it's convenient isn't a connection. It's a convenience, not love. It's a favor economy. A loyalty sale. A one-sided subscription service with no renewal benefits.

You're not a vending machine. You're not here to be pushed only when someone wants something to come out. You're a full human being, heart, soul, flaws, laughter, and all. You deserve the kind of care that shows up unannounced, that checks in without needing anything, that loves you when you're useful and when you're just you.

You are not a backup plan or plan B. You're the whole damn plan. The people who see that? Keep them. The rest? Let them miss your magic when they remember you again.

Learning to Breathe Through the Unbearable

Tonight, I lie in my bed with a heavy heart and a troubled mind.
I wonder if life's trials are making me bend or break.

I know I'm stronger now; I can feel it in my bones.
But still, my mind won't rest, not after what you did.

And yet, tonight, my heart rides a different wave,
caught in the tide of emotions and terrible memories I wish I could forget.
These troubled waters aren't ready to meet me at the shore.

So I wait... until the waves settle and silence holds me again.
Maybe then, I'll feel like myself.

Until then, I breathe.
And slowly, I learn to accept the unacceptable.

The Things Most People Miss

I never see the big picture. While others are focused on the whole story, I get caught in the small, passing moments most people don't think twice about. The way someone avoids eye contact when they say they're okay. The pause before a forced laugh.

A shift in tone that's barely there but still says everything.

I don't mean to notice. It's not something I try to do. But I do. Every time. Even when I wish I didn't. Maybe it's my Virgo zodiac thing, or maybe it's just survival. Something I never got to grow into.

I was born with it. Knowing how to read the room before the room reads me. Wired to tune into the things people don't say out loud. I'm not looking for signs or trying to dig deeper. It just happens. Like my mind is scanning the edges of every conversation, catching what slips through the cracks.

Even silence feels loud to me. I catch the pauses, the shift in energy, the way certain words are avoided like they might crack something open. Most people let those moments pass. I can't. They stick with me. The tension. And no matter how much I wish I could unsee, unhear, unfeel, it has already buried itself somewhere deep. That's the curse. I always see too much. And I remember.

The tiny details. Everything. It stays with me, even long after the moment's gone. Even after the person who dropped it forgets they ever did.

It's not about wanting to be right, or seen, or needed.
It's deeper than that.
More lonely.

It's feeling the weight of things unspoken and knowing you can't ask about them without breaking something.

And carrying the emotional leftovers of a moment that didn't belong to you but somehow still does.

Sometimes I wonder if it would hurt less to be oblivious. To just smile, nod, and not feel the things no one says out loud. And there are days I wish I could unlearn this. Wish I could pass people by without picking up their pieces.

But that's not how it works. When you notice everything, you end up holding more than you're meant to. And most of the time, no one even knows you're holding it.

The Ache That Comes After the Echo

There's a moment when it all sinks in. Not with some dramatic meltdown or tears-in-the-rain kind of collapse. It just settles in your stomach like a weight you didn't ask for. Wraps itself around your ribs and makes itself comfortable.

It's not just the ending that hurts.

It's the space afterwards. The stillness. The way certain corners of your life feel hollow now. The laughter that used to live there? Gone. Your phone used to light up with their name, now it just stares at you like it's waiting for someone who isn't coming. Even your own name feels off, like it's missing something ever since they stopped saying it.

You start replaying things you know you shouldn't. Conversations that felt endless. The way they looked at you was like you made sense. Promises tossed out in passing that meant more than either of you wanted to admit.

It's not just remembering. It's your body still reacting like they're here. Your mind keeps reaching for something that isn't there, like muscle memory refusing to get the message.

And honestly, it's not even the heartbreak that sticks. It's the fear that maybe you won't be able to do this again. Worse, it's the fear that maybe you could have made it work if you'd just done things differently.

Said the right thing. Shown up when it mattered... that maybe it slipped through your hands and it was on you.

And now you're stuck holding a story that never got its ending, just all the pages where it started to feel real, and the ache of knowing you still would have chosen them, even now, even after everything. And you keep wondering if they ever look back, if they ever miss you too, like you miss them. But that's the thing. You don't get to know that anymore.

Happiness Moves

The world's a big, beautiful place, far too full of wonder to live the same day on repeat. So try something new. Go somewhere you've never been. Let new places teach you things. Talk to strangers. Real conversations can turn into real connections. Let small moments catch you off guard, make you smile, remind you you're alive.

Fall in love, not just with people, but with sunsets that make you pause, street food that tastes like magic, and the thrill of not knowing exactly where you're headed but going anyway.

Happiness doesn't wait. It dances through movement. Laughter that bubbles up for no reason. Stories shared with people who get it, while a bonfire glows and the night stretches wide open.

A taste that lingers, makes you close your eyes and smile.

Happiness isn't careful. It's wild. Fun. Really live your life.
Say yes to the unknown. And never stop exploring.

The Price of Peace

When you finally choose peace, it often comes with a lot of goodbyes. And not the loud, dramatic kind you see in movies, just necessary ones. Sometimes it means letting go of people you thought would be in your life forever. It means walking away from conversations that used to keep you up at night. It means no longer chasing after people who only come around when it's convenient for them.

Choosing peace means choosing yourself, and that decision doesn't always make sense to others. You might lose friendships. You might disappoint people. You might even feel lonely at times. But eventually you realize, it isn't about having everything go perfectly. It's about finally breathing easy, even if that means standing alone for a while.

Peace asks for space. It asks for honesty. And more often than not, it asks for distance from chaos, from conflict, from anything that costs you your sanity. You'll start to notice how still the world becomes when you stop fighting battles that were never yours to begin with.

And in that stillness, you'll begin to heal. Not all at once, but piece by piece. The truth is, peace doesn't just show up. You have to choose it. And choosing it means learning how to say goodbye over and over again to anything that doesn't feel like calm.

Forever Etched in My Soul

I'll never forget the people who helped me when I was falling apart.

Those who saw me at my lowest and didn't turn away, even when everything felt dark and still.

They didn't just say they cared; they showed it again and again.

They stayed with me when I had nothing to give. Gave me strength without asking for anything in return. Held space when words didn't work. Offered light when I couldn't find my own.

What they gave wasn't just kindness; it was healing. It didn't just help me get through, it reminded me how to believe again.

Those people? They're more than memories. Their love, loyalty, and spirit are part of who I am now. No matter where life takes me, they'll always be with me forever carved in my soul.

Weight I've Known Before
(Healing Group Journal)

Someone from my healing group asked me the other day,

"How do you keep moving forward when everything feels so heavy and unbearable?"

And I didn't have to think long.

I said,

"This weight isn't new to me. I've carried worse. I've held pain in my chest so deep it made it hard to breathe and I've moved through days that felt like they wanted me to gone. I've been shattered. Alone. Emptied out completely. And still, I made it through."

So when life tries to crush me again, I remind myself: I've already survived storms that were supposed to break me and walked through hell without anyone even knowing I was burning. If I made it out of that? Then there's nothing left that can finish me.

The Funeral You Never Saw Coming

You're not just leaving him. You're saying goodbye to the version of you who begged for love from someone who was never capable of giving it the way you needed.

This isn't just about being heartbroken. It's a funeral for the girl who waited by the phone, who tried to be more lovable, more easygoing, more patient while he gave her the bare minimum and acted like it was everything.

You're grieving the part of you that made excuses for his silence, that held onto hope like it was all you had, that truly believed if you just stayed, he'd finally choose you.

But he didn't. He couldn't. And now you finally see it wasn't about you not being enough. It's just who he was. And realizing that shatters something deep inside.

When the Feast Begins

You learn a lot when everything falls apart, when the lights go out and the silence weighs a ton, and you are left holding yourself together with nothing but raw willpower and stubborn hope, and that is when the truth pulls up a chair, uninvited, unfiltered, and brutally honest. You suddenly see who is really in your corner, who checks in without being asked, who listens without trying to fix you, who simply stays, and just as clearly, you see who disappears without a word.

Some people cannot handle your storm, and that is fair, but the truth is, some never even tried, they bailed the moment your life stopped being fun, convenient, or Instagrammable, and all of a sudden, it is crickets, no texts, no calls, just a vanishing act so complete it deserves an award. And strangely enough, that is a gift in disguise, Those hard moments work like filters, brutal, yes, but effective, and they strip away the fake, the fair-weather friends, the ones who only stick around when you are shining and easy to love, and they make space for the real ones.

So when the healing begins and your soul starts to bloom, when your life starts to look like the comeback tour it was always meant to be, remember this, when your table is overflowing, when the feast is in full swing and the air is filled with laughter and warmth, you do not owe a seat to anyone who left you hungry, and not everyone deserves a plate just for showing up when things are good again, or suddenly deciding they miss you.

You are allowed to protect your peace like it is fine china, to take roll call with clear eyes, and to never forget who walked away when all you had to offer was pain, Gratitude doesn't require amnesia, and forgiveness doesn't mean handing out second chances like party favors.

Let your table be filled with love and with the people who stood in the rain with you, whether they had an umbrella or not, and let your joy be shared with the ones who saw your mess, your chaos, your grief, and showed up anyway, the ones who never needed perfect to love you well.

And as for the others?
Wish them well, but from the driveway.

Silent Battles We All Face

Every now and then, we find ourselves in battles no one else can see. Not the kind that unfold with shouting or slammed doors, but the ones that live in the soft corners of our minds and the heavy spaces we carry in our hearts. These are the struggles that rise in silence, behind steady breaths and tired eyes, the ones we face alone and over and over, even when we're already worn thin.

We smile when we'd rather vanish. We keep our hearts open in a world that constantly gives us reasons to close them. We extend forgiveness that's never asked for. Not from pressure, but we know what it feels like to carry around pain so heavy it hardens us. That kind of strength doesn't get applause. It isn't loud. But it's real. And it's brave.

There's no celebration when we choose grace instead of rage. No medals when we stay soft in a world that dares us to go numb. But we continue. These battles might not leave visible bruises, but they settle into the body, in the tension in our shoulders, in the weight that lingers long after the moment has passed, in the steady ache that surfaces when everything else goes still.

They shape us, slowly and deeply, shifting how we move through life, how we protect what matters, how we begin to guard our peace like something sacred. And even after everything, we do not shut down. We reach for calm when chaos feels justified. We love even when shutting down seems safer. We let ourselves hope, even with no promise of what's ahead. That is strength, the kind that doesn't need a spotlight to matter.

We fight these private battles in small, ordinary moments. The kind where we fall apart behind a bathroom door, then pull ourselves together before anyone notices. The kind where we whisper encouragement just to make it through the next step, the next breath, the next hour. These moments go unseen by the world, but they are everything. They are where our real power lives, steady, gentle, unwavering.

And we're not doing this for applause. Choosing compassion isn't easy, we just know what the alternative feels like. Something in us still believes we don't have to turn into what hurt us.

Healing's still possible, even with the pain, and peace doesn't vanish just when things are loud. And turning bitter? That's not who we're trying to be. We're building something stronger. Something rooted.

Maybe the world will never fully understand what we carry or how many times we've had to pull ourselves out of the dark. But the fact that we are here, continuing to try, continuing to hold on to who we are? That is the kind of brave the world does not always recognize, but desperately needs.

She Faced the Past to Move Forward

She touched the past, not to mourn it, but to grow beyond it.
There were days when the weight of old memories felt like too much to carry.

Mistakes she made, things she lost, people who walked away, and versions of herself she no longer recognized. All of it lingered in the background. For a long time, she avoided it, pretending it didn't matter. She smiled, stayed busy, shared only the good parts of her life, and buried the rest deep inside.

But eventually she realized healing doesn't come from hiding pain. So she stopped running and began to face it, one piece at a time. Not to relive it or stay trapped in it, but to understand and learn from it.

Revisited the moments that hurt the most, but instead of letting them break her again, she used them as proof of how far she'd come. Forgave herself for the choices she made when she didn't know better. Let go of the need for closure from people who were never going to offer it. She stopped wishing the past had played out differently and started focusing on creating something better ahead.

Touching the past didn't make her weaker. It made her wiser. And now, when she looks back, it's not with regret, but with respect. She survived it. She grew through it. And she's still growing. So yeah, she didn't touch the past to stay in it. She touched it so she could move through it.

You Said There Was No One Else

You looked her in the eyes and told her there was no other woman, just you and your family. She asked you more than once. Not to accuse. Something felt wrong, and she couldn't ignore it.

And still, you said no. You denied, deflected, and dismissed her concerns as if they didn't matter. You made her feel like she was overthinking, being paranoid... insecure.

But she wasn't.

When you came back, the truth wasn't hidden. It was right there, she saw it by accident, on your phone, in a picture that said everything your words wouldn't.

Her, with you. The one you swore on your father's grave was not there. It's not just a lie. You broke the trust she gave you, the faith she had in your word, and the safety she thought you both shared. You had a choice:

To be honest, own it and face her with respect. But you chose deceit.

A Soft Hello, A Braver Heart

When you meet someone new, it's like turning a fresh page in a story you didn't realize was still being written. There's a spark of possibility, a gentle hope that maybe, just maybe, this connection will mean something: a lesson, a turning point, or perhaps a kind of healing.

You carry your past, of course. All the love you gave, the heartbreak you survived, the pieces of yourself you've been carefully putting back together. But in that moment, there's a pause. A stillness. The world shifts ever so slightly, and a soft question lingers in the air: Could this be something good?

It might begin with a simple hello, followed by shared laughter, deep conversation, and the way their presence makes the world feel a little less heavy. And in those moments, you feel your heart stir again.
Carefully.
Cautiously.
But with hope.

You don't have to know what it will become, not yet. Maybe it's just a flicker. Or a new beginning of something beautiful.

Either way, meeting someone new reminds you that you're still capable of opening up. Worthy of connection with the possibility of love.

A Strength of Yours

You've finally let go of the pressure to be perfect, to always achieve, always perform, always prove something. That version of strength, the one that never slows down, never breaks, never admits it's tired, isn't real. It's a mask you were taught to wear. But it doesn't hold. It never did.

Real strength looks different. It's softer. Steadier. More honest.

It's knowing when to pause. When you need rest, not guilt, when caring for yourself doesn't feel selfish, just necessary. It's being able to say, "I need a moment," and honoring that moment like it matters. It does. Strength isn't about pushing through at all costs; it's about knowing when to put something down when it's too heavy.

You're learning to feel what's actually there: grief, anger, sadness, confusion, loneliness. You don't suppress those feelings or pretend they don't exist. But you don't let them take the wheel either. You sit with them. You listen. You learn what they're trying to say.

And then, like storms, you let them pass. They do pass. And behind all of it, the sky remains, unchanged and whole.

You don't have to become every emotion you feel or fix everything and have all the answers right now. You just have to keep showing up, honest, human, open.

A Thousand More Tomorrows

I couldn't save you. I held you, I loved you with everything I had left in me. I wanted you to stay. And then, I had to let you go.

Grief hurts. It sneaks up and steals your peace when you don't expect it. It doesn't wait for permission or give a warning. It just arrives, in a breath, in a memory, in the space you left behind, and suddenly nothing feels steady anymore. A part of me was lost in that fragile moment caught between your life and your death. And no matter how far time moves, I keep going back to that place, to the second everything changed, and I couldn't stop it.

I needed more time. More time to memorize every line of your face, to hold your hand, to make the moment last just a little longer. To hear your laugh echo in the air as if it might circle back to me. To lie beside you, whispering in the dark with you, holding on to the closeness before it faded into absence.

I needed a thousand more tomorrows and a thousand more "I love you's." I just needed more time with you.

With love, as always,
Bella.

Art in Motion, Strength in Words
(Healing Group Journey)

Reflection of Annam
Written by Annam Healing Group members

She doesn't speak much these days, but when she does, her words can lead to deeply intelligent conversations if she wants them to. She's a thinker, with her coffee, her pen, and her music.

She wears black clothes like armor. That's her style. And there's something so deep in her eyes, it makes people stop and stare. She doesn't even realize it, but she has a power, a kind of power that doesn't need to shout. Her soul is beautiful, and she's not afraid to be different. Pain cannot stop her. She is art and an artist at the same time.

Someone in our group once quoted her:
"Hurt an artist, and you'll witness masterpieces born from the damage shared with the world."

But with her, it's something else entirely. Her written words don't just cut; they carve.

Deeper than any blade, deeper than betrayal. They don't just echo pain. They make you feel it.

Her strength is in her pen, her courage in her words. She writes for the ones who feel too much, for the ones who are lost, hopeless, to remind them: they are not alone.

Cost of Truth

When you speak the truth, you don't just make noise. You make enemies. And no one warns you about the price tag. There's no receipt, no return policy. Just fallout.

People love the idea of honesty. They wear it on shirts, post quotes about it, and act like it's the moral high ground. Until your truth rattles their comfort. Then suddenly, you're "too much," "negative," or "bringing drama." What they actually wanted was the digestible version.

Truth in lowercase. Polished. Pleasant.

Preferably with a smile.

But truth doesn't play nice. It doesn't come tied up in a bow. It kicks the door in. It doesn't calm the water. It capsizes the whole boat. And when it does, people jump. You lose, folks. Not just acquaintances, but people you loved. People who swore up and down they were your "safe space" but disappeared the second your truth stopped being convenient.

Turns out, they didn't want honesty. They wanted you to edit. Softer. Easier to handle. The version of you who smiled through it and made things smooth for them. When you stopped being that person, they walked away like you were the problem. Like your honesty was the betrayal, not the years you spent swallowing your voice.

But the biggest loss? The part of you that believed truth would bring closeness. That it would fix or heal things. You thought being real meant finally being seen. Instead, you were met with distance. Cold shoulders, people slowly backing away once they realized they couldn't rewrite your story. And it shifted something in you.

Maybe it was pride, peace or maybe just the wild clarity that, for once, you chose you.

Anyway, the truth didn't set you free like all the Pinterest quotes promised. But it did something better. It made you honest. And even if it's lonely, it still beats fake and surrounded.

Every Day Brings Another Story

It starts off as a joke. The casual way he walks through the door, tossing his keys into the bowl, saying with a smirk, "Another woman hit on me today."

Maybe the first time, it was amusing. The second time, curious.
But when it becomes a daily ritual, it stops being funny and starts feeling like an invasion.

Underneath those repeated stories is a question he never asks but always implies: Are you still impressed by me? Do you still think I'm wanted?
And maybe, even more hauntingly: Do you still feel lucky to have me?

Each time he shares it, you're forced to absorb it. Smile politely. Laugh, maybe. But inside, a seed of unease grows. Not from insecurity. No. You know your worth. But this isn't about admiration anymore. It's about attention. It's about control. It's about planting doubt under the guise of honesty.

So here's the truth you hold in your chest but never say out loud:

If he needs daily validation from strangers more than he needs emotional security at home, then he's not the one who should be bragging. He's the one who's already lost something.

If your presence isn't enough to make him feel seen, then your absence needs to be the loudest silence he's ever heard.

End of story.

Finding Her Voice in a Foreign Tongue
(Third-Person Self-Reflection)

When she was younger, she moved to another country, thinking she was simply changing her address, packing up clothes, books, habits, and dreams into neat boxes. But the moment the plane touched down, she realized she had also left behind something more: the invisible infrastructure of who she was.

Suddenly, everything she said carried an accent. Every opinion felt like a question. Even silence, once comfortable, grew louder. She struggled for words, translated herself before speaking, and watched conversations slip away like trains she couldn't catch. She used to be articulate. In her native language, she had rhythm, humor, and certainty. Now she was awkward, overly cautious, almost mute.

She didn't realize how much of her identity was built on communication until she was stripped of it. The world misread her, and she began to misread herself.

But there was an unshakable kind of strength in that dismantling. She started listening more. She started learning not just a new language, but a new self. Piece by piece, she found ways to be heard again, not just in another tongue but in another life. And in the silence between words, she learned to become someone she had never dared to be.

Someone who is publishing her fifth book in a language other than her native one.

The Ones Who Go Anyway

Written the only way it can be by someone who didn't get to imagine the worst. Just survive it. She could be anyone. No names needed. Just the facts only someone who lived it would know.

She grew up in a house where nobody listened. Doors got kicked in. Plates got broken. Learned early that if she didn't move fast enough, someone's rage would find her. And it always did. Her stepfather hit her for things she didn't do, and even harder for the things she did. Her mother never stopped him. Just turned up the radio. Nobody came to stop it. By the time she was eleven, she already knew how to lie about her bruises. Didn't tell anyone what went on in that house.

The food was locked. Not just hidden. Locked. A chain on the cupboard. A padlock on the fridge. She wasn't allowed to eat unless they said so. And they almost never did. Used to press her ear to the kitchen door, listening for the sound of them leaving so she could try to sneak a crust of bread. Sometimes there wasn't even that. Hunger stayed. Not the kind that fades. The one that rewires your body.

She learned to go long without food, safety, kindness. Learned not to cry. Crying made them meaner.

By thirteen, she couldn't take it anymore. Ran without shoes. No plan. No goodbye. Just ran until the trees opened and the village was gone behind her. Lived on the street. Slept behind buildings. In stairwells no one used. Stole food and clothes. Didn't want to. But it kept her alive.

Then winter came. She got sick. Got cold. Bruises came from places that didn't hit the way home did. Kept her head down and moving. Didn't wait for help.

By fifteen, she had figured out how to survive. How to spot danger from down the block. Read people before they spoke. Kept going when her body screamed for rest.

Found work eventually. Small things at first. Cleaning rooms. Washing dishes. Jobs that paid just enough to keep her standing. Saved every bit. Kept it folded inside a sock she wore at night. Months passed. Then more.

Got a small room. More like a shed. No kitchen. No furniture. Just four walls and a lock she owned the key to. First time in her life she could close a door and breathe.

Worked hard. Harder than most people ever do. And not just to eat. Worked to feel human again. Learned how to budget. How to look people in the eye without flinching. Put her life in order piece by piece, with her own hands. As the years went, moved to another place and finally stood on solid ground. Still, didn't rest. Just turned around.

Found a way to help others still living the life she had fought to leave. Refused to walk past people stuck in the kind of hurt she had crawled through.

So now she goes. With others who know what it means to walk toward the worst of it. They go where very few ever will. Where it's dark. When it looks past saving in everyone else's eyes. Where the room's already shattered, the door's been broken for months, and the screams have stopped and silence has taken over. They go.

Don't wait for anyone to come looking. Move through halls. Lift children still in pajamas. Pull women out barefoot. Grab a bag. Unlock a door. Carry who needs carrying. Then disappear before the world even notices someone is missing.

One of them went bad.

They had gotten the woman out, and one of the kids. The other was still asleep upstairs. Everything had been timed. She was halfway up the stairs when the headlights cut across the window.

No one said anything. No one had to. Moved faster. She grabbed the boy. Wrapped him in a blanket. Didn't let him wake up all the way. She was almost to the front door when keys hit the porch. They couldn't all make it out. Not fast enough.

Told the others to run. One of them hesitated. She didn't. Just pushed the boy into their arms and turned back toward the hallway.
He came in angry. Sharp. Grabbed her by the neck and shoved her into the wall. Asked what the hell she thought she was doing. She didn't answer. Just bit her lip to stay silent.

Tasted blood. Tasted rage. He slammed her again. Didn't know there were others. She didn't let it show.

He hit her harder the second time. Something cracked. Didn't remember falling. Just landing. Her back hit the floor, and the lights above her spun. He stood over her, breathing hard, calling her names she had heard before. Ones that didn't touch her anymore. Closed her eyes and waited for the next one. It didn't come.

Last thing she heard was one of hers yelling. When she opened her eyes again, he was gone. The others had come back for her when they realized she hadn't come out. Helped her to her feet. Told them she was fine. But she couldn't lift her left arm. Said it was just bruised.

Went to another house two days later. After everything. With the aches that don't heal right. They had gotten everyone out. That's all she cared about. Pain passes. But not showing up when someone needs you... that doesn't. She just wants to do what's right and make sure when someone is finally able to ask for help, there's a pair of hands reaching back. Even if those hands shake later or bleed.

There's no story told at the end. No medal, headline or thank you. Just children sleeping in a warm bed for the first time in ages. A woman who doesn't have to explain the bruises on her body anymore. For them, no words needed. They feel it. In the way she looks at them and stands between them and the door.

When some ask her how she does it.
She doesn't answer. Just remembers what it was like to be a child, waiting for someone who never came. Then she gets back in the car.

Doesn't speak to other people about what happens in those moments. It's not redemption or trying to make sense of what happened to her back in time. That part never made sense. What she knows is there's never enough time or enough hands. That's why they keep showing up anyway.

Yet there are times she comes home shaking from what she saw and couldn't unsee. From what someone tried to do. To her. To the others. To the ones they went there to pull out and they arrived just a few minutes late. No words can explain that.

Imaginary Visitors
(Self-Reflection)

In my younger years, I used to imagine things going wrong. Why? I was so lonely, and I just wanted to know if someone actually loved me, even if it was only in my mind. I wanted to know that if something ever fell apart, someone would notice, that I wouldn't just slip away, unnoticed and unmourned. That I was not just a lost cause, but worth the effort.

Looking back, it breaks my heart to realize that, as a child, I so often mistook imagined pain for closeness. I didn't know how to ask for love. I only knew how to hope someone might sense the need I couldn't name.

And no one did.

But over time, things changed. I began to understand that love doesn't always arrive through grand gestures.

Sometimes it shows up in simple ways, through good people, kind strangers, and steady friends. The ones who check in for no reason. The ones who stay.

And maybe more than anything, I learned to show up for myself. To sit with my own sorrow and learn from it. To become the person who stays, even when no one else does.

I'm not that lonely kid anymore. I still have hard days, but I no longer wait for imaginary visitors.

I've become someone who sees the parts of me I used to hide and lets others see them too.

Inside Your Mind

Everyone thought she would fall apart. He had broken her down in front of others, unapologetically, smiling as if watching her fall confirmed something twisted he believed about himself. They whispered about the silence that followed. How she didn't lash out or throw back words like blades.

Instead, she went still. But in that silence, something else began to take shape.

She came to understand that shooting back would be pointless. No punishment she could imagine would exceed the one he already lived with each day. His voice, laced with venom, still echoed. He had taken her tenderness and spun it into something weak, made her love feel foolish, her softness something to be ashamed of. And when the anger faded, replaced by a deeper ache, a thought surfaced.

Someone who could be that cruel to a person who only ever tried to love them must be far crueler to themselves. That idea didn't offer comfort, but it revealed something. It moved beyond the sting, below the hurt, and into a still place where understanding took shape, not as an excuse, but as a kind of clarity. If he treated her with such malice, then the storm inside him must be far worse than anything she could wish upon him.

As it settled, she began to look deeper, not just at what he had done, but at the reasons he might have done it. People don't destroy something good unless they're already losing a war with themselves. And though she didn't pity him, the weight lifted. In that letting go, she recognized the truth: the guilt he carries will outlast the pain she feels for trusting him too long.

She does not forgive him or excuse him or refuse to soften what he did, but forgives herself for staying too long, for loving too hard, and for carrying what was never hers to hold in the first place.

She walks forward now, free. The pain has lifted, as she no longer carries his.

Keep Going, Even When It's Hard to See Where

Life has a way of shifting, whether we're ready or not. It moves forward, with or without a plan, and somehow, we keep moving too. Not that it's easy, but that something inside us says, "Don't stop now."

Happiness doesn't always show up the way we expect. It's not always tied to achievement or certainty. Sometimes, it sneaks in softly, in the middle of a walk with no destination, in the laughter of someone who was a stranger an hour ago, in a song you haven't heard in years. It lives in the trying. In the tasting. In the not knowing.

You don't have to have it all figured out. You don't need a map to move forward. What you do need is that bit of courage that says, "I'll go anyway."
And if you've ever felt like you don't fit, like the way you see or feel things is too much for the world, don't shrink. You were never meant to blend in. You were built to break the mold, to ask different questions, to walk a path only you can see.

Some people won't understand that. They'll suggest you tone it down, play it safe, take the easy road. But the world doesn't change simply when people play it safe. It changes when someone like you keeps showing up fully, even when it's uncomfortable.
And when things fall apart, since they will sometimes, you don't have to pretend to be okay. You don't have to smile through it. Let yourself feel it and sit in the mess for a moment. That doesn't make you weak. It makes you human.

The truth is, no one has a perfect run. Life brings storms. Pain. Setbacks you never saw coming. But strength isn't in pretending they don't hurt. It's in choosing to keep moving anyway. To stand back up, even when your knees shake.

So take the road that's yours, even if it's the long way, the strange way, the one no one else understands. Let the world be big. Let it change you, surprise you.

One foot in front of the other. That's it. You're still here, and that's enough, and it's exactly where your story continues. Don't rush the next chapter. Let it come when it's ready. And while you wait, live, not perfectly, just honestly.

Let It Hurt

When your heart breaks, don't you dare go into hiding.
Don't smother it with forced smiles or bury it under endless distractions. Don't dress it up in spiritual slogans or pretend you're above the pain. Let it split you open if it must. Let it sting, ache, and humiliate you a little. That's not a flaw in your wiring. That's the beginning of healing, and no, it doesn't come with a user manual or a deadline.

Feel all of it. Cry so hard your face forgets how to hold shape. Scream into a pillow, or into the air, or just in your head if you're somewhere public and don't feel like being escorted out. Sit on the floor and do absolutely nothing for two hours. That counts as surviving. This is your pain, not a group project. No one gets to vote on how you handle it.

People will show up with opinions, sometimes wrapped in concern, sometimes just noise. They'll suggest yoga or journaling or lemon water. They'll say things like, "Stay positive," or "Everything happens for a reason," as if your heartbreak is some kind of cosmic lesson in disguise. You don't have to accept any of it. Their words might come from love, or habit, or discomfort. Doesn't matter. This is not their grief. This is yours. And only you know what it feels like to wake up missing someone whose absence rearranged the furniture of your soul.

You don't need to be okay right now. You're allowed to fall apart in your oldest sweatpants, eating dry cereal straight from the box at 3 a.m. with one sock missing while the light's off. To ghost everyone, cancel plans without explanation, scroll like you're searching for something but don't know what. That's all part of it, too.

So don't rush to disinfect the wound. Let it linger a while. Let it burn and change how you walk into rooms, how you trust, or carry your joy. That hollow space inside? It's not just emptiness. Its space being cleared for something else. Maybe not today, maybe not next month. But eventually, that space might start to grow something worth keeping.

And today, even if all you managed to do was sit on the edge of your bed and stare at the floor, that's enough. When nothing makes sense, when everything stings, when hope feels far away, that doesn't mean you're broken. That means you're human. That's what healing looks like in real life. It is not poetic. It is not pretty. But it is real.
Let it hurt. All the way through.

Once You Realize the Power of Your Presence, You Won't Just Be Anywhere.

There comes a moment in life when you finally understand the weight of your presence, what it means to show up, to take up space, to bring your energy, your heart, your truth into a room. And once that moment comes, everything changes.

You stop giving your time and energy to places, people, and situations that don't honor who you are.

You become more intentional, more aware. You begin to protect your peace, value your worth, and carry yourself with an unshakable confidence that doesn't need to be loud to be felt.

Once you realize that your presence is power, not just your words or your actions, but simply you, you stop showing up just anywhere. You stop shrinking, settling, or trying to fit into spaces you've outgrown.

You start walking into rooms with purpose, and you stop apologizing for taking up space. You learn to choose environments that see you, feel you, and respect what you bring.

And from that point on, you don't just go where you're invited. You go where you're valued.

Real Confidence Doesn't Beg for Attention

Ever notice how the loudest people in the room are usually the ones trying the hardest to prove something? They talk over everyone, stir up drama, and constantly need to be seen. But most of the time, that's not confidence. It's insecurity in disguise.

Here's the thing:
When you really know who you are, what you've been through, and what you stand for, you stop needing to explain yourself all the time. You stop trying to impress people and pretending to be something you're not.

Real confidence is calm. It doesn't need applause.
It doesn't fall apart when no one's watching. People who are truly confident don't chase attention. They show up, hold their ground, and let their energy speak for them.

But insecurity? That's loud. It feeds off drama and validation. Hiding behind moodiness or fake happiness.
It covers up fear with those things hoping no one notices what's missing underneath.

When you're solid in who you are, you don't waste your time proving anything. You just live it. And that's what makes you strong.

Rotten Fruit Always Looks Ripe at First

It always starts the same way. The face looks like a blessing, the words sound holy, and the whole vibe is just shiny enough to trick people into thinking it's the real deal. At first, everything seems golden: loud laugh, big presence, knows how to light up a room like they invented charm. But magnets? They pull you in until you realize you're stuck to something already rusting.

And somehow, this one always ends up in the middle of everything. Offering to help, handing out support like its candy, ready with the ride, the tissue, the speech. Not as though they care but given that being useful is their favorite disguise. It makes them feel needed, wanted, like they matter. And when there's nothing left to fix and the emptiness creeps in, they go looking, sometimes in places that were never theirs to touch.

In the beginning, it works. People gather, entertained, comforted, fooled just enough to stay. They've got jokes, they've got drama, they've got just enough fake wisdom to sound deep at brunch. But it doesn't last. The same crowd starts backing off slowly, like they just smelled the truth. And once they're gone, the whispers start as things don't just fall apart for no reason. The unraveling always comes with flattery that feels too polished, stories that shift every time they're told, and a mess that somehow never belongs to the one who made it.

The emotions? Perfectly timed. Crying in 4K. Smiling like nothing's wrong while something's rotting underneath. And sympathy? Collected like reward points. Just enough pain shown to earn pity, never enough truth to spark real questions. People who stay long enough start to feel like background characters in someone else's tragedy parade. And the prize you thought you were holding? Turns out it was empty the whole time.
People catch on. You feel it in the silence, the space, the way your name comes back wearing clothes you didn't give it. That shine that once felt magnetic now leaves a mark.

Not that it burned too bright, it just never burned at all.
And still, somehow present in every drama that isn't theirs. First on the scene, front row for pain that doesn't belong to them, carrying other people's grief like it earns them a crown. That role, the rescuer, the helper, the one who's always there, is just a distraction.

Back home, nothing's fixed. The walls are thin. The mirror won't lie. Misery loves to stay busy.

But the truth doesn't stay hidden forever. Ashes don't lie. And when the applause runs out, when no one claps anymore, the same question floats to the surface: "Why is everyone against me?" Yet maybe it's not everyone. Maybe kindness stitched out of emptiness doesn't hold up in bad weather. Maybe the costume was never convincing to begin with. Maybe people just finally stopped pretending they couldn't see it.

So just call it what it is: Some people try so hard to play the hero, they forget the whole cast already spotted the zipper down the back of the suit.

She Left to Remember Who She Was
(Self-Confession)

After they returned, she told him she wasn't going back to him anymore. Couldn't. Not after what he told her. That terrible thing he did. The pain was deafening.

Not a soft ache or a heavy longing, but a constant scream in her chest.

The wound was so loud that she had to leave the country. Not for a vacation or chasing adventure.

She needed to leave, since it was impossible to breathe without drawing in those words, she never asked to hear.

Every corner held a graveyard of mental pictures, which was never hers to carry. No path without running into ghosts. No sleep without dreaming of the horror he confessed, by accident.

So she left, not for a new life, but for a moment of stillness.
A chance to feel something other than him echoing in her ribs.

She stepped away to remember who she was before love became survival. Before mistakenly being chosen for being safe. Before forgetting how to belong to herself.

And maybe, to begin the impossible work of learning how to love herself louder than the pain he left behind.

Where is she now?
She's not healed. After knowing that horrible thing of his, she's not whole. But she is away. And for now, that's enough.

Simple Way Forward

Someone once asked me how I'm able to walk away from family, friends, even a partner when they've shown me they aren't who they claimed to be.

And honestly? It was never some big, dramatic moment. It was quiet. Heavy. But clear.

Every time something like that happened, it felt like standing at a crossroads. And I had to ask myself: who's truly meant to keep walking this road with me? Who's shown they can come along, and who's already shown me they can't?

It's not about being cold. It's about being honest.

When someone lies, manipulates, or turns on you, they've already stepped off your path. You're just choosing not to chase them.

You don't beg people to treat you right.
You don't carry betrayal into your next chapter.

Some goodbyes don't echo. They just... need to happen.

It stings, then it settles. And one morning you wake up, make your coffee and somewhere between the first sip and the last, you realize you didn't check the door waiting for them to call and show up different or tearing yourself apart trying to make sense of it.
You just find other things to care about.

Starting Over Isn't Starting From Scratch

Don't be afraid to start again.
This time, you're not going back to square one.

You're moving forward with all the baggage... I mean, the wisdom you've picked up along the way. You carry the lessons, the scars, the wins, the cringe-worthy mistakes, the heartbreaks that had you listening to sad playlists on repeat.

You know what hurt, what broke, and what made you stronger (eventually).
Starting over now means starting from experience. You're older, wiser, a little more cautious, and somehow even braver (yes, you).

So don't let fear boss you around. It's perfectly fine to fall apart, just don't unpack and live there.
Remember: you've already survived what once felt impossible.

The Climb and the Fall

What breaks people the most is realizing how fragile everything they've built really is. How hard it is to climb up, and how easily it can all collapse. You can give your all, fight through every obstacle, spend years working on yourself, your dreams, your healing, and still, in a single unexpected moment, it can slip away.

That's what leaves people reeling. The climb demands everything: patience, strength, resilience. But the fall? It's instant. No warning. No mercy. Just like that, they're back at the bottom, questioning whether they have it in them to rise again.

What cuts even deeper is when the fall doesn't just erase progress. It takes pieces of them, too, pieces they may never get back.

So every climb becomes more than a journey upward. It's an act of courage. They're carrying not just their hopes but the weight of everything they've lost and still chosen to rebuild from.

The Night You Don't Remember
(Third-Person Self-Reflection)

You don't remember that night. Or deep down, you're trying not to. Maybe it's easier that way. Easier to bury it somewhere out of reach, where it doesn't sting so sharply. But that night was real. It still exists, just beneath the surface, no matter how much you try to forget.

That night changed everything. It wasn't just what happened. It was what you said. Not by mistake. Not in passing. You meant every word, and afterwards, she was left shattered. She felt like something inside her had split wide open, bleeding in places no one else could see. Even the people who might have wished her harm, if they had seen her then, really seen her, would have stopped.

Maybe even dropped their hate for a moment. Maybe they would have held her and they would have cried. When someone is that broken, that visibly undone, even the cruelest people recognize the weight of it. The truth of it. And they flinch.

It hurts to revisit that night. The silence it left in her. The ache of being utterly alone while surrounded by people who had no idea what you said or what she was carrying. Perhaps that's why you won't remember. Remembering means facing it. Feeling it. The fear. The shame. But forgetting doesn't make it vanish. The scars are still there. Just hidden. Just hers.

The Noise Means Nothing.
Your Journey Means Everything.

The loudest critics? They're usually the ones who paid nothing to get in. Cheap seats, cheap opinions. Funny how the people who never lifted a finger to support you somehow feel very qualified to tell you what you're doing wrong.

They weren't there for the sleepless nights, the breakdowns, or the brutal self-work it took just to stand upright.
They didn't offer love, time, or understanding, but now they're self-appointed experts on your life choices?

Please.

They mock your ambition, question your motives, and throw shade at your progress. It's easier than facing their own regrets. Your growth exposes what they've been running from. This was never about your path. It's their discomfort.

And let's be real:
Anyone can sit on the sidelines and boo. It costs nothing to run your mouth from a place you've never had the guts to leave.

So let them.
Let them project, gossip, and post their passive-aggressive nonsense. Their opinions only gain weight if you decide to carry them.

Instead, listen to the ones who showed up when you were all heart and no resume. The ones who clapped when no one else was watching. The ones who didn't need proof to believe in you.

That's your circle. That's your crew. That's who matters.
The rest? Background buzz with strong opinions and zero receipts.

You were never meant for the sidelines. You're the main act. So keep building the life they said you couldn't. And make it loud enough that even the cheap seats can't pretend they don't see it.

Too Late for Sorry

You said you were sorry, but by then the damage had already been done. Not just recently. It had been building for a while. And it didn't just pass through me like a storm; it stayed. It made itself at home.

Your apology felt soft, maybe even sincere. But it didn't land the way you hoped. The thing is, by the time those words came, the hurt had already settled in. It had already changed me. I wasn't the same person who used to wait for you to make it right.
What you broke didn't disappear. It lingered. It found places in me I didn't even know were there. It unpacked. It made itself comfortable. It rewrote the way I love, the way I trust, the way I see you.

Pain doesn't always scream. Sometimes it whispers. Sometimes it sinks in slowly and silently. It reshapes you in ways you don't notice until you've already changed. That's what your actions did. While you moved on easily, I was left behind, collecting pieces of myself, trying to move forward with a heart that didn't beat quite the same.
I'm not saying your apology meant nothing. I know it probably cost you something to say it. But some wounds go deeper than words can reach. Sometimes we don't need the past erased. We just need someone to finally understand the weight they left behind.

Yes, I heard you. I really did. But your "sorry" reminded me of everything I've spent so long trying to forget. And by the time you said it, the pain had already unpacked its bags. I'd already learned how to carry it on my own.

Unsent Letter to You

I should be grateful; I was the last voice you heard, the last person you spoke to, the final breath of sound before everything went silent. But I'm not grateful. I'm angry, angry at myself. I wasn't enough to save you. I didn't know how to hold you in a way that kept you here. I've replayed it over and over, the words I said, the ones I didn't.

As if maybe, if I'd just said the right thing, the perfect thing, you'd still be breathing. Somehow, my last words weren't enough to anchor you here. I couldn't conjure a miracle. And my voice didn't rise like a spell.

I wanted my voice to be magic, to be a lifeline, to be louder than the darkness that swallowed you. But I was just me, fumbling, terrified, helpless, loving you the only way I knew how. It wasn't enough. And I hate that the last thing I gave you wasn't a miracle. It was just my voice shaking, soft, and breaking as I told you you'd be okay, even though I didn't believe it.

I'm sorry for every moment I couldn't change, for not being a God when you needed more than a person. And still, even now, if you somehow hear this, if your soul still lingers near, know this: I loved you. I love you still. And I would have carried you out of the fire if I could. I would change places with you. But all I had were words.

And I hope you heard in them everything I couldn't say out loud, that you weren't alone, even as you let go. People tell me to cherish it, the final call, that sacred moment. Yet all I hear is everything I didn't say. All I feel is the echo of you slipping away.

With love, as always,
Bella.

We All Bleed Differently.
But not in The Same Way.

Some bleed through pain you can see, in bruises, tired eyes, and aches etched across their body and face. Life hits hard, and those marks don't lie.

People notice immediately. They ask what happened, and you have the words to answer.

Others bleed in ways unseen: silent battles no one knows about, moments when fear stops them from speaking up or standing tall, even when their heart desperately wants to be heard. But the truth stays hidden, buried beneath the weight they carry alone.

Many hold their pain inside, not with bandages, but in the way they behave. Quick to anger, shutting down, throwing themselves into work, keeping others at a distance, pretending everything is fine.

Pain doesn't always announce itself loudly. Sometimes it lingers in stillness, tucked away in what's left unsaid. You sense it in small talk, when someone pulls away, avoids eye contact, or uses humor to mask what they truly feel.

Yet pain is pain. Whether it's visible on your skin or concealed behind a smile, It's human. Beneath it all, everyone carries wounds.

When He Realized I Was Completely Crazy
(But It Was Too Late)

At first, he thought I was just quirky. You know, harmless weird. Like "talks to plants," weird who "has a playlist called Songs to Stalk Your Houseplants To."

But then
He saw me argue with the GPS like it had personally betrayed me, since I never pay attention, and I'm always lost. Then, I cursed out a toaster as if it intended to burn my toast. He caught me dancing in the street and narrating the neighbors' lives like a full-blown soap opera, complete with plot twists and suspicious recycling behavior.

"And I love her for it," he thought. "That's my girl."

He didn't even flinch when I explained the conspiracy theory that the mailman was a secret news reporter secretly gathering all the neighborhood gossip, and honestly, he was the one who always brought me the freshest updates.

He didn't even blink when I named every pothole on the street.

He just laughed, full-body, eyes-crinkling, chest-shaking kind of laughed, and said, "God, you're ridiculous.
And I'm ridiculously in love with you."

Poor guy never stood a chance. He'd already fallen, fluent in my chaos.

Addicted to the sound of my laughter after ugly crying, the way I get defensive when I'm scared. Already knew I love too much, talk too fast, repeat myself constantly, and cry when I'm angry since rage feels too loud in my chest. He loved the way I danced badly, which spoiler, was not entirely on purpose.

Chose me, every version, every volume, every meltdown, like it was the easiest thing he'd ever done. He knew I was broken but loved me more for that.
Seen all my wreckage and stayed anyway.

He called it beautiful chaos.

I called him a certified lunatic, the only one crazy enough to survive my level of madness. He loved me like I was the most normal thing in the world. And that's how I knew it was real. Anyone can love you when you're easy. But he stayed through the broken, the messy, the loud.

Through the "what the hell is she doing now?" version of me.

And now?
Now he's gone. The angels called him home.
And suddenly, everything is more still.

I don't argue with the GPS anymore, since there's no one beside me to tease me when I get us lost, no one to reroute with a happy smile. No one tells me to stop crying at 3 a.m. commercials or kisses the crazy right off my forehead when my well-hidden insecurities flare up.

P.S.

You stayed when you didn't have to, when letting go would have been easier.
Even now, long after you're gone, there are no refunds, no exits, no way to undo what was.
Just so you know, a part of me still dances like an absolute fool, convinced you're watching me from heaven, secretly impressed, and maybe a little terrified, as you mutter, "Oh no, here she goes again."

Thank you for loving me, and choosing me, even with all my chaos.

Love as always,
Bella.

When the People Closest to You Try to Undermine Your Relationship

Sometimes, the biggest problems in your relationship don't come from your partner. They come from the people around you. Friends, family, even people you thought had your back, can say or do things that slowly chip away at your connection.

They start planting doubts, making little comments, and reminding you of your past. Questioning your partner's every move. Pointing out every flaw based on what they know from the edited version you told them.

They stir the pot, then act surprised when things go wrong. Maybe they're jealous. Maybe they don't like your partner. Or maybe they just can't stand seeing someone have what they don't.

They might act like they're "just being honest" or "looking out for you," but deep down, you know the truth. It's not about concern. It's about control.

They want to stay on the pedestal they built in your life. And your relationship threatens that. Someone else is getting your heart and your attention.
And that scares them.

My advice:
You truly need to reflect on why no one has ever been good enough for you in their eyes and why no one ever will be.

You must recognize the selfish motives behind their actions. They've never been satisfied, not with a single person you've welcomed into your life, unless they're the ones who choose them for you.
Or your person bows their head for them.
And deep down, I think you already know this.

But also, sometimes you're the biggest problem. You carry shame about those things you did behind the scenes, and you left out the parts that made you look bad. Figured playing the saint was easier than owning what you did.

Where Dreams Begin to Breathe

This is for a very special girl, as in between her words, I heard something rare: truth without armor, beauty without trying.

For you, Mayra.

Someone I hold close to my heart, who's no longer with us, once told me something that changed the way I see life:

"Dreams become reality when your thoughts turn into actions."

I didn't grasp the full weight of those words at the time. But life has a way of teaching us through struggle, small victories, and those moments when giving up feels easier than holding on. Dreams are more than wishes. They are pieces of your soul, shaped by hope, carried by longing, and silently waiting for you to believe in them enough to begin. But dreams don't come alive through thought alone. They need movement, courage.

Even the smallest step taken with intention has the power to shift your entire world. There will be days, hard ones, when you feel like you've given all you have. Days when the light within you dims, and your body and heart ache from trying. When the weight feels too heavy, give yourself permission to pause but not to give up.

You are not weak for needing rest. You are human. Breathe. Let silence hold you for a while. Let your heart mend in the stillness. Then rise slowly, gently, with whatever strength you've found. The dream is still there. It hasn't left you.

And every time you choose to keep going, even after breaking, you bring it closer to life. This is how dreams begin to breathe, not through grand gestures, or perfect timing, but in the sacred decision to keep moving forward.

Love,
Bella.

Why Don't You Be the Bigger Person?
(Healing Group Journal)

Why don't you be the bigger person and reach out?

That's what people often ask me when they don't know the full story.

But here's what they forget:
Being the bigger person doesn't mean tolerating disrespect, excusing someone's insecurities, or reopening wounds that took time to heal. It doesn't mean sacrificing your peace to revisit pain just to make others more comfortable, nor shrinking yourself to fit back into spaces that once broke you.

Sometimes, being the bigger person means recognizing when a relationship, be it a friendship, family tie, or anything else, is no longer healthy, when your effort goes unreciprocated.

When you're constantly being put down so someone else can feel better.
Sometimes, being the bigger person means walking away. It means choosing silence over chaos, jealousy, insecurity, and malice.

Distance over damage. Self-respect over one-sided loyalty.
It means knowing when something is no longer good for your soul and loving yourself enough to let it go.

Why Him

After his funeral, someone asked me,
"Why him? Why choose someone you knew wouldn't be here for long?"
Why?
For the reason that he never cared about the fancy clothes I wore or the perfectly styled hair. He didn't fall for the polished version of me, the one who looked like she had it all together.

What truly mattered to him was the real me: the me on sleepy mornings, with no makeup, messy hair falling where it pleased, in simple clothes that felt like home, smiling big when he woke me up with coffee. He saw my soul in those soft, unguarded moments and loved me deeply for it.

He found beauty in my simplicity, my bare skin, my tired eyes, the way my voice cracked mid-laugh during our late-night whispering in bed. He called that beautiful.
On the days I felt worn out, when I barely recognized myself in the mirror, when I felt least deserving, he told me I was radiant. He noticed the light in my smile, the sparkle in my eyes when I talked about something I loved, and the way my nose crinkled when I laughed too hard. And whenever I told him to focus on his work, worried that I was distracting him, he would smile gently and say, "Doing that as we speak, amore mio, just keep talking to me."

To him, hearing my voice was the sweetest part of his day. It was his comfort, and nothing else could compare. My presence, even messy and imperfect, wasn't a distraction to him. It was his grounding force.

He didn't need me to be flawless. He just needed me to be me. Messy. Crazy. Real. Yappy. And in a world that kept asking me to be more, he made me feel like I was already enough.

That's why it was always him. Not due to how much time he had left, but on account of how we filled the time we had.

With love, as always.
Bella.

Why I Stay Silent
(Healing Group Journal)

People from my healing group often ask me why I don't do anything, why I don't defend myself, why I don't speak up. So many whys... but...

The answer is simple: it's freeing. I know the truth, and that's enough for me.

At one point, they were my friends, or at least, I thought they were.
And even after everything that happened between us, I still won't throw dirt on anyone.

Not that they don't deserve it, but I refuse to stoop to that level.
But let's be real. I'm still human. There are days when the anger rises. When I feel rage and want revenge.

When I want to scream my side of the story so loudly it shakes the truth out of everything. But then I stop. I take a breath. And I realize I don't need to do that. I don't need to help them dig their own grave deeper.

Not in some effort to be the bigger person. Not out of kindness or nobility. No. It's that they're already doing it themselves.

They are perfectly capable of ruining their own lives, and they do it effortlessly, without any help from me.

They're living with shame, no matter how hard they try to pretend otherwise.
And some things are better left in the shadows, not to protect me, but to protect them.

At the end, it's not my problem anymore.

And you know what?
There's a kind of peace in that.

Why She Seems Cold

You asked why she seems cold, why it doesn't feel like she cares anymore. It's simple: Her heart gave up trying to keep her alive in a situation that was slowly killing her. And that situation... was you.

She used to feel everything. Love, hope, pain. Gave too much. Held on, even when it was tearing her apart. And it broke something inside. The mind started slipping, so the heart took over.

It said, "I'll carry this pain, so she doesn't lose herself." And it did, until it couldn't anymore. It shut down so she could keep breathing. Now, not much reaches her. Not from a lack of desire to feel...

Her heart had to die a little for her mind to survive you.

You Were the Apology and the Crime

No one really understands what it's like to be both the crime and the apology, to be the one who somehow hurts someone and then gets expected to fix it, even when you never meant to break anything.

You got stuck in that cycle, carrying blame like a weight you never asked for and never deserved. Whenever something went wrong, the fault always found you first, like you were the only one who could make things fall apart, even when all you were doing was trying to survive.

You started to believe you were the problem, that your feelings were too much, your words too loud, your presence a mistake. So, you said sorry. Again, and again. Even when your heart was breaking. Saying sorry felt safer than telling the truth. Safer than facing someone's anger crashing down on you like a storm.

But being sorry didn't stop the hurt. It just made you smaller. It made you shrink until you barely recognized yourself. You became the apology, a soft voice whispering "I'm sorry" before you even knew what you were sorry for. And somehow, you were still the crime too, the reason the air got tense, the silence filled the room, the broken piece nobody wanted to claim.

It's a lonely thing, being blamed for wounds you didn't cause. Carrying guilt that was never yours. And the hardest part? Believing that if you stop apologizing, everything will fall apart. That your silence will be the proof that you really were to blame.

You got tired. Tired of being both the crime and the apology. Tired of the cycle where your pain didn't matter, where your voice always had to soften, bend, and beg for peace. But in time, you learned: constant apologies don't heal anything. They just keep the hurt buried deeper, heavier.

You're Part of My Story,
But Not the Whole Book

You're part of my story, yes, that's true. You were there during a chapter that changed me. Maybe you hurt me. Maybe you helped me. It could have been both. But no matter how big your role was, you don't get to be the whole book. You were a part of the plot, not the main character. You were in a lot of scenes, even in a few seasons, but this story, this life, still belongs to me.

You don't define who I am. Showing up during a hard part doesn't give you control over how my story unfolds. Just since you once lived in my heart doesn't mean you get to stay in my mind forever. And although something happened doesn't mean it owns me. Yeah, I felt broken for a while, but that doesn't mean I'm still that person.

I've lived through things that shook me, changed me, and even brought me to my knees. But I didn't stay there. I pulled myself back up. I grew. I learned. I healed in moments no one else even noticed. There's so much more to me than what happened with you. You're a page in my past, not the title of my life.

I don't need to hate you, erase you, or pretend you never mattered. I can honor the fact that you were there, that it meant something, while still choosing to move forward without you.

I just need to remind myself that I'm still writing. I'm still living. My story didn't end there. It didn't freeze in that moment. I kept turning pages, even when it was hard, even when it hurt.

So no, you don't get to define me. I do. Every single day, I wake up with the chance to write something new. Something better. Something that has nothing to do with you at all.

Closing Chapter:
The Last Page, Not the End

It's strange how life moves, how we carry on after things we thought would break us, and then, without realizing it, we adapt. We grow and learn how to live with what we've been through, not by forgetting it, but by letting it become part of who we are.

This journey wasn't clean or easy. There were moments of doubt, missteps, and long silences. But you made it here. That matters more than anything.

You don't need to prove your worth to anyone. You've already done the hardest thing: you faced yourself, and you kept moving. That alone is enough.

As this book closes, don't see it as a finish line. Let it be a pause, a space to take a breath. You've come a long way. You've earned the right to rest, to reflect, to just be.

What comes next is yours to decide. Not everything needs to be figured out right now. It's okay to take your time.

This isn't the end.
It's just where the page turns.

Love
Annam.

You'll Find Strength Where You
Were Shattered

www.ingramcontent.com/pod-product-compliance
Lightning Source LLC
Chambersburg PA
CBHW052330100426
42737CB00055B/3304